ACKNOWLEDGEMENTS

• •

Major thanks to my mum and dad for all you've done. We are talking MAJOR thanks here. Thanks also to Karen with an e for your inspiration, the guided tour of BT2 and endless supply of *Cosmopolitans*, without which the girls in this book would be, like, TOTALLY naked.

I owe SO much to, like, Ger Siggins, who edited and produced these memoirs with a passion and drive completely at odds with the remuneration he will receive. And he, like, came up with my name and shit.

Admiration, man. Also, roysh, I have to say a big thank you to *Sunday Tribune* editor Matt Cooper, for your brave, undercover, reconnaissance work in the hospitality tents down at Lansdowne Road and for all the support you have given me.

Oh, and for having soul, man. I am, like, SO grateful to Vin, Rich, Lise with an e, Fleur (!), Ró and Jimmy for your suggestions and proof-reading skills. Any typos are, like, down to you, goys. Many thanks to Bret Easton Ellis for the inspiration. And finally, MAJOR gratitude to Dublin Bus. Thank you for the 46A, a rich source of material. And we're talking total here.

For my mother and father,
for teaching me the
difference between
right and Ross

This book is a work of fiction.
Any similarity between any of its characters and real people,
living or dead, is purely coincidental.

First published in 2000 by *The Sunday Tribune*,
15 Lower Baggot Street, Dublin 2, Ireland.

ISBN 0-9526035-8-6

Designed & edited by Gerard Siggins

Cover by Jon Berkeley/God's Holy Trousers
Artwork by David Gorman
Back cover photograph by Lar Boland

Printed by Colour Books, Dublin

THE MISEDUCATION OF ROSS O'CARROLL-KELLY

as told to Paul Howard

1
●●●

CASTLEROCK BOARDERS ARE TOTAL SPAS is scrawled in, like, blood red lettering on the side of the bus shelter outside Stillorgan Shopping Centre, roysh, and is in print large enough to be seen from the passenger seat of the old dear's car as it lurches forward in traffic and just as I notice the words, roysh, a bus pulls up, an advertisement for Calvin Klein jeans on its side blocking my view, but I don't care because I tell the old dear to turn up the radio, and it's like, 'The Drugs Don't Work' on FM104, and the old dear, a total spa herself, ignores me.

I'm like, "I am SO totally late" but she, like, totally blanks me again.

I know what it's about. Last week, roysh, the old man found out that I've been skipping my grinds. I haven't, like, gone to one so far. He had a major freak-out. We're talking MAJOR here.

My Christmas report came, roysh, and I failed, like, six of my seven exams and at first he was like, "Don't worry, Ross, it's not your fault. I'm going to phone the Institute tomorrow and find out what's going on."

I'm like, "Don't do that."

He's like, "I'm paying two thousand pounds a year for those grinds, Ross. It's quite obvious the teachers aren't good enough."

I'm like, "Well, I wouldn't know. I've never been."

When he heard that, roysh, he went, like, totally apeshit. We are talking total here.

He goes, "What on earth have you been doing every Friday

night and Saturday morning."

I goes, "Hanging around town."

I didn't tell him I've been, like, in the pub with the goys because he'd have a total eppo. So him and the old dear haven't been talking to me for the past, like, three days, roysh, but I don't care because the Schools Cup storts in two weeks and they'll be, like, all over me then. We're talking TOTALLY here.

The goys are already sitting in Eddie Rockets when I arrive. Oisínn's wearing beige Chinos by Dockers, brown Docksider shoes by Dubarry, a light blue Ralph Lauren shirt and a red, white and blue sailing jacket by, like, Henri Lloyd.

He stands up and gives me a hug and shouts "YOU THE MAN, ROSS" a few times in my ear. JP high-fives me from where he's sitting. JP is wearing beige Chinos by Dockers, brown Docksider shoes by Dubarry, a light blue Ralph Lauren shirt and a red, white and blue sailing jacket by, like, Henri Lloyd. I'm wearing beige Chinos by Dockers, brown Docksider shoes by Dubarry, a light blue Ralph Lauren shirt and a red, white and blue sailing jacket by, like, Henri Lloyd.

Aoife leans across the table and, like, air-kisses me on both cheeks. She's a total flirt. Sorcha, my ex who is, like, first year Orts UCD, stares at me and she's like, "We've already ordered."

Oisínn is like, "Question for you, Ross. Now if anyone can answer this, you can."

I'm like, "Go on."

He's like, "Is it proper to wear Docksiders with formal wear?" I'm like, "How formal is formal?" He goes, "Black trousers, white shirt, black blazer." I rub my chin and think about it.

The food arrives, roysh. Oisínn is having the Classic with no dill pickle, southern fried chicken tenders, bacon and cheese fries and a large Coke. JP is having, like, a Moby Dick, chilli fries, a side order with nachos with guacamole, cheese sauce, salsa and hot jalapenos, and a vanilla malt. Sorcha is having a Caesar salad with extra croutons and Romanie lettuce.

Aoife is having a bag of popcorn, which she has hidden inside her Ralph Lauren red sleeveless bubble jacket. She's, like, constantly looking over her shoulder every few seconds, roysh, and she's like, "I have to be careful. Me, Sophie, Caroline, Suzanne, and Deirdre got thrown out of the one in Donnybrook last week, because we only ordered a milkshake between us." Sorcha says that this is "SO unfair".

The waitress, roysh, is a total babe. We are talking TOTAL here, roysh, and she comes back and she's like, "Do you want anything." I'm there, "What I want and what I get are probably two different things" and she goes totally red, roysh. Totally. She's definitely into me. I can see Sorcha out of the corner of my eye and she's, like, giving her daggers. I'm like, "I'll have the Dolphin-friendly tuna melt, a chili cheese dog and a portion of buffalo wings," and she smiles at me and goes off, roysh, and Sorcha's like, "That girl is a TOTAL spa."

I'm like, "Who is she?"

And Aoife's like, "Sian Kennedy. She's doing morkeshing in ATIM."

I'm like, "What does ATIM stand for?" and JP's like, "Any Thick Idiot with Money" and I laugh and, like, high-five him.

Aoife kicks him under the table, roysh, and she's like, "It stands for Advanced Technical Institute of Morkeshing and I'm focking going there, so watch what you say."

JP's like, "Hey, man, I was only joking."

I'm like, "Is that a diploma course?"

And she goes, "No, it's a degree. Well, a degree from the University of Rangoon, but my dad's company will recognise it."

Then she's like, "They'd better. It's, like, eight grand a year."

Oisínn goes, "Ross, you never answered my question?"

I'm like, "What question?"

He's like, "Docksiders with formal wear. What do you think?"

I measure my words carefully. I'm like, "Well guys, the Docksider is traditionally a casual shoe."

I look at Sorcha, who's, like, stirring JP's chocolate malt with a straw. Then she takes a sip of it.

Oisínn is like, "But the Docksider has become acceptable just because it's so popular?"

I'm like, "Yeah, but to be worn with formal clothes, they have to be black and red."

"What about brown?" JP asks suspiciously.

I think about this, and then I'm like, "Too sporty for black trousers. Beige trousers definitely. Black, no way."

Then Sorcha's mobile goes off, roysh, and it's, like, Jayne with a y, who's, like, her best friend, or used to be until she caught her snogging with me in Fionn's house on New Year's Eve. Sorcha had a total knicker fit and, like, finished with me.

Anyway, her and Jayne with a y are obviously back talking again, roysh, and they're going on about some dinner porty they're, like, organising together.

All of a sudden, Sorcha's like, "Is Fionn there with you?" I turn to the goys, roysh, and I'm like, "What's the story with Fionn and Jayne?"

JP's like, "They're going out together." Which is, like, news to me, because I've been seeing Jayne with a y for the past four weeks, roysh, and she asked me to keep it quiet while she tried to, like, patch things up with Sorcha. What a total bitch.

Sorcha is, like, really enjoying it. She's like, "Ross, I've got Fionn here on the phone. He's going out with Jayne now. He wants a word."

And she, like, hands me the mobile, roysh, and Fionn is like, "Ross, I want to ask you something."

I'm like, "Shoot."

He's like, "If you're wearing a tie with a blazer, which knot looks best?"

I sigh and, like, run my hand through my hair, which needs a serious cut, especially with the Schools Cup storting in, like, two weeks. I might get a blade one all over this time instead of, like, just at the sides.

I'm like, "That's a good question. Are we talking drunk or sober?"

He's like, "Either."

I'm like, "Well, among people of our age, the blazer is associated with a smart yet casual, preppy look, but it's actually a versatile piece of apparel. With a blazer, I would have to say that a four-in-hand knot is most appropriate, and that's whether you're wearing a pinned or unpinned shirt collar."

Then I'm like, "That's when you're sober anyway. But knowing you, after two pints of Heino, you'll have the thing tied around your head, and a traffic cone under your arm, you focking spa."

Then I, like, snap the phone shut, roysh, and throw it across the table at Sorcha.

She's like, "Oh my God, Ross, you're not jealous, are you?"

I'm like, "Yeh roysh."

Then I'm like, "Been there, seen that, done that."

She was, like, totally freaking when I said that.

Then the waitress comes over with my order, roysh, and I'm like, "Is your name Sian Kennedy?"

And she goes, "Yeah."

And I'm like, "You're first year morkeshing in ATIM, aren't you?"

She's there, "Yeah. I think I know your face. You go to Annabel's, don't you?"

I'm like, "Yeah. Maybe I'll see you there this weekend."

She's like, "Yeah, totally."

I'm like, "Cool."

And she's like, "Bye."

And I'm like, "Yeah, bye. I'll see you around."

We're talking TOTALLY gagging for it here. Oisínn high-fives me.

Aoife's like, "Oh MY God, you don't fancy her, do you?"

I shrug, roysh, and I'm like, "She looks like Kelly out of *90210*."

Aoife's like, "Yeah, but she's a total spa. We're talking total here, Ross."

Sorcha was having a major knicker-fit at this stage, roysh. Majorly jealous. She turns to Aoife and she's like, "So, do you think I should go?"

Aoife's like, "What?"

She's like, "Do you think I should go?"

Aoife's like, "Oh my God, you SO should go."

I, like, totally ignored it, roysh, but then JP, the total retard, he turns around and he's like, "Go where?"

Aoife's like, "She's been invited to the Bartholomew's pre-debs."

Oisínn's like, "By who?"

And Aoife's like, "Jamie O'Connell-Keaveney."

Sorcha's staring at me, looking for a reaction. She's only doing this because she knows we have Bartholomew's in, like, the first round of the cup.

JP is like, "That is SO not cool, Sorcha. That is SUCH an uncool thing to do."

Sorcha goes, "Why?"

Oisínn's like, "Why? HELLO? Bartholomew's are our total enemies."

JP nods and he's like, "They're total spas."

Sorcha goes, "Jamie isn't like that. He's totally cool."

And Aoife goes, "What do you think she should do, Ross?"

I shrug my shoulders and, like, pop a piece of tuna into my mouth. I'm like, "If she wants to go, that's cool. She should do whatever makes her happy."

Oisínn's like, "But not with somebody from Bartholomew's."

JP's like, "Oh MY God, we are SO going to kick their orses now." JP and Oisínn high-five each other.

Then Aoife gets up, roysh, and she goes into the toilet. JP's like, "I cannot BELIEVE she's going to the toilet again. That's three times since we arrived." Oisínn swears blind that he can taste dill pickle and he, like, takes the top bun off his Classic to investigate. He's like, "What does she need to go to the toilet for anyway. It's not like she ever focking eats anything."

Sorcha tells the goys not to be mean. She takes off her scrunchy and slips it onto her wrist, shakes her head, smoothes all her hair back into a low ponytail again, puts it back in the scrunchy and then pulls five or six strands of hair forward. I don't understand why she does that. It looks exactly as it did before she did it. Aoife returns from the toilet, calls one of the other waitresses over and asks for a glass of, like, water. The waitress asks whether we want, like, dessert and shit. Oisínn and JP order the Kit Kat dream. Sorcha orders the New York toffee cheescecake with cream and ice cream.

Aoife's like, "Oh MY God. Do you KNOW how many calories are in that?" Sorcha shrugs her shoulders but looks as though she regrets ordering it. The waitress looks at me and I, like, shake my head and stand up to leave.

JP's like, "Ross, where are you going?"

I'm like, "Home."

I walk up to the counter and tell Sian what I had and she, like, adds it up. I hand her a tenner and tell her to, like, keep the change and then say that I might see her on Friday night and she smiles and says that's cool. Behind me, I can hear Oisínn telling the rest of them that he can definitely taste dill pickle on his burger and there's, like, no way he is going to pay for it.

He's like, "I am TOTALLY not paying."

Aoife shouts out, "We'll see you Friday night, Ross. Annabel's."

I totally blank her and go outside. I cross the road to the bus stop, where there's these two girls waiting for the 46A, total skangers, one of them telling the other that Sharon, or Shadden, is a fucking dirtbird. I'm definitely going to sit downstairs. I take out my mobile and, like, listen to my messages. Some girl called Alyson phoned. She said she hoped I remembered her from Saturday night, that she couldn't remember whether I was supposed to phone her or she was supposed to phone me tonight, but she decided to call anyway, and if it's after midnight when I get this message I should phone her tomorrow, but not in the morning because she's at the orthodontist, and she gives me the number again.

* * * *

I'M, like, already awake when the old dear comes into my room.

She's like, "Ross, it's half past eight."

I totally ignore her, roysh.

She's like, "Ross, it's half past eight."

I'm like, "I FOCKING SAID I ALREADY KNOW."

And she's like, "Ross, don't use that kind of language to me. I'm just saying you're going to be late for school."

I'm like, "No shit, Sherlock."

Then she, like, focks off downstairs. Total retard.

Oh MY God, I need a serious shower this morning. My hair and my face are all, like, SO sticky, and they smell of, like, orange. I feel around the floor and find my dark blue 501s and my blue Chaps jumper with the US stars and stripes on it and they, like, smell of orange as well. Sorcha threw a Bacardi Breezer all over me in Annabel's last night. She totally freaked out when she saw me with Sian. And we're talking totally here.

I didn't bother my orse going out on Friday night. Treat them mean and all that. A couple of the goys were out. We're talking Simon and Fionn, and they said Sian was, like, asking where I was. Totally gagging for me.

15

On Saturday night, I ended up in, like, the Wicked Wolf in Blackrock. Simon and JP called around last night and asked was I going out, so we went for a few scoops in Donnybrook and then ended up in Annabel's. The second I went in, I spotted Sian up the bor, roysh, trying to play it cool but totally looking over. She was with a couple of her mates and they were, like, SO obviously talking about me. I played it totally cool, roysh, ordered a pint of Heino and, like, chatted with the goys for about half an hour, then, like, moseyed on over.

Sian was totally cool with me. We're talking totally here. I'm like, "Hi" and she's like, "Hi".

I have to say, roysh, she looked totally amazing. She was wearing a black strapless mini dress by Morgan, black pony mules by Karen Millen and a black leather jacket by Lawrence Steele. I introduced myself to her two friends. Melissa was a complete babe but Olwen was, like, a total dog. Melissa was wearing a white mini dress by Fenn Wright and Manson and sandles by Gucci. Olwen was wearing a black gypsy top by Prada, black trousers by Calvin Klein and boots by Gucci. One, or maybe all three, was wearing Tommy Girl.

Sian was still, like, totally blanking me, so I storted flirting with Melissa.

I'm, like, "You used to go to school in Killiney, didn't you?"

She's like, "Oh my God, how did you know that?"

I'm like, "Because you did *West Side Story* with the sixth years in our school last year."

And she's like, "Oh MY God, I am SO embarrassed. Total shamer." Then she's like, "Are you still in Castlerock?"

I goes, "Yeah."

She goes, "Oh my God, do you know Jamie McIvor?"

I'm like, "Yeah."

She's like, "Oh my God, I'm taking him to my debs."

I'm like, "He is totally sound."

She's like, "Oh my God, I can't believe you know Jamie McIvor."

Then she's like, "So, who do you know in Killiney?"

I'm like, "Elinor Snow. Amie Gough. Bryana Quigley..."

She's like, "Oh my God, you know Bryana Quigley."

I'm like, "Yeh, I was with her during the summer, twice."

She's like, "Oh my God, she's one of my best friends. I can't believe you know Bryana Quigley."

This must have, like, made Sian really jealous, because all of a sudden, roysh, she turns around and storts talking to me.

She's like, "I didn't see you down here on Friday."

I'm like, "No, I was practicing my kicking."

Melissa's like, "Oh MY God, you're on the rugby team?"

I'm like, "Yeah."

Sian, roysh, she gives her this, like, filthy look, and Melissa's like, "Em, me and Olwen are going to go and look for Esmé. See you later."

Sian goes, "She is SUCH a focking bitch."

I'm like, "She seems sound."

She's like, "She's my best friend. I think I know her better than you."

I'm like, "Sorry."

She's like, "You couldn't trust her. She is SUCH a sly bitch. She KNOWS that I like you."

I'm like, "Do you?"

Then she goes, like, totally red, roysh, and she's like, "Yeah, but you already know that."

I'm like, "Don't be embarrassed. I've liked you for ages."

She's like, "Really?"

I'm like, "Yeah." And I ended up with her, roysh.

Next thing, I open my eyes and who's standing there, only Sorcha. She was wearing a pink Ralph Lauren shirt with the collar up, a white body top, black jeans by Diesel and black loafers, I think, from Fabio's in Blackrock Shopping Centre. She was also wearing Allure by Chanel. Anyway, roysh, she totally flipped.

She was like, "It didn't take you long, did it?"

I'm like, "Sorcha, you were the one who finished it."

She goes, "And you've moved on already."

I'm like, "That's it, yeah. Onwards and upwards."

She's like, "Yeh, roysh. I'd hardly call that onwards and upwards."

Sian's like, "Sorry?"

Sorcha's like, "You heard."

And Sian goes, "Who the fock do you think you are?"

Sorcha's like, "I'm Sorcha Lalor. And I know all about you and where you're from. Collars Up, Knickers Down."

I'd, like, just taken a mouthful of Heino at that stage, roysh, and I, like, nearly spat it all over the place.

I'm like, "Oh yeah, the Whores on the Shore."

Sian's like, "Well, it's better than the Virgins on the Rocks" and then she turns to me and gives me this filthy, roysh, so I knew I had to, like, get rid of Sorcha.

I'm like, "Look, Sorcha, you broke it off with me and as far as I'm concerned, you did me a favour. We're both free agents now, so just get over it."

Then she, like, throws half a Bacardi Breezer over me.

Her friends dragged her away then. We're talking Aoife and Nikki, who's, like, repeating in the Institute.

They're like, "He's not worth it, Sorcha."

Sian's like, "I can't BELIEVE you went out with that total knob."

I'm like, "I don't want to talk about her. I only want to talk about us," and we storted, like, kissing again. Anyway, I ended up spending half the night with her, roysh, and got her phone number at the end of the night. I promised her I'd ring her on Tuesday night, but I'll probably leave it until, like, Friday.

Anyway, I'm feeling, like, totally shabby this morning, and we're talking totally. One or two too many scoops, I'd have to say. I have a shower and put on my black 501s, my All Blacks jersey and my brown Dubarry Docksiders and head down to the kitchen. I open the fridge and grab a carton of, like, milk and drink it.

The old dear's like, "Ross, I've told you before not to drink milk straight out of the carton."

I'm like, "Mum, I'm 18 years of age. I'm not a kid anymore, alroysh?"

She goes, "I know you're not a kid, Ross. That's why I can't understand you keep acting like one."

I'm like, "Shut up, you total spa."

She's like, "Ross, you don't have your school uniform on."

I'm like, "No shit, Sherlock."

The thing is, roysh, we don't have classes this morning, because Sooty – Mr Sutton, the coach of the S – is giving us all a talk. He says the game against Bartholomew's is, like, the toughest first round draw in the history of Castlerock and we're going to have to, like, seriously get our heads down.

The old dear drops me off, roysh, and she's like, "What time will you be home?" and I totally blank her. I meet a couple of goys outside the assembly hall – we're talking Terry, Newer and Gicker – and we head in and everyone's, like, already there, roysh.

Sooty's like, "Heavy night on the sauce last night, lads?" and everyone's, like, breaking their shites laughing.

He's like, "No, lads, in all seriousness, I want to say to you what I've just been saying to the other guys. We can't underestimate Bartholomew's. They are serious players. Gone are the days when they were considered the poor relation of the Schools Senior Cup competition. They have a great team this year. If you win this game, I guarantee you won't have a more difficult match until the final. So what I'm saying is that I want you guys to get your heads down for the next week or so, lay off the sauce, lay off the late nights. I've spoken to your various teachers and you're all excused from homework for the next fortnight."

We're all like, "YYYEEESSS!!!"

He's like, "That gives you space to concentrate on the job in hand, do your gym work, focus on your own game."

We're all sitting in, like, a circle, roysh, and he goes around asking us, one by one, what our expectations are.

Fionn is like, "I guess to make everyone in the school proud of me".

Newer is like, "Well, the school has a lot of history behind it, especially in the Schools Cup. I guess I'd like to become part of it."

JP is like, "I want to win the cup so the old man will buy me a Golf for my 19th."

We all, like, TOTALLY crack up.

Sooty's like, "No, guys. It doesn't matter what your own personal motivation is, as long as you are focused on winning the match in hand." Then he turns to me, roysh, and he's like, "What about you, Ross?"

I, like, don't say anything, roysh.

Then he's like, "Ross, what are your expectations."

I look up, like, really slow, shrug my shoulders and then I'm like, "Kick ass."

And the whole place goes totally mental. Everyone is, like, standing up on the tables and, like, screaming and cheering, and shouting "You the man, Ross". I look over at Sooty and he's, like, standing on his desk at the top of the room, punching the air with his fist over and over again, and shouting "Come on. Come on. Come one."

* * * *

JP grabs my arm and, roysh, and he shakes me, and he's like, "Ross, are you alroysh?"

I'm like, "Yeah."

He's like, "I asked you can you hear them."

I'm like, "Who?"

He goes, "Our supporters."

I'm too focused to hear anything, roysh, but then I listen carefully and I can, like, hear them outside the walls. They're like, "We will, we will, Rock you, fock you, anyway you want to."

Me and Simon, who's like, our captain, roysh, we gave a little speech at choir practice yesterday, just, like, telling them how much their support means to all the goys and, like, how we have to totally frighten the life out of the opposition today. JP has storted crying and Simon is hugging him and, like, telling him to calm down and focus. Gicker high-fives me. Terry and Newer are, like, standing with their foreheads pressed together and they're, like, screaming at the top of their voices, "LET'S FOCKING DO THEM! LET'S FOCKING DO THEM!" Oisínn has gone totally apeshit, roysh, and he's, like, punching the wall – his hand is in total ribbons – and he's like, "WE'RE FOCKING CASTLEROCK. CASTLE-FOCKING-ROCK."

The speech that Father Feely, who's like the school president, gave us at assembly this morning has, like, totally fired us up for the game.

He was like, "We're making this year the Year of the Eagle. The eagle is the strongest and cleverest of all birds. He soars through the skies. Majestically. He rules the air. And I'd draw an analogy between the eagle and the students here at Castlerock. You are the élite. You are better than everyone else in the whole world and the success of the school's rugby team is an expression of your superiority over other schools, particularly schools for skangers."

I had tears in my eyes at that stage, roysh, and then he's like, "The perpetuation of the purity of our race depends on you. It is vital that the eagle proves just how dominant he is, before you all go off to work for investment banks that fuck up the Third World or management consultancies which close down factories and throw poor people onto the dole."

I looked around, roysh, and all the goys – we're talking Simon, Fionn, JP, Oisínn, EVERYONE – was bawling their eyes out. Then all the goys on the S were made to, like stand up and walk up onto the stage and everyone's, like cheering and screaming and crying, roysh, and we all sing the school anthem, *'Castlerock Above All Others'* a couple of times. It's, like, SUCH an amazing song. It was written back in, like, the 'Thirties and it's like:

Castlerock boys are we,
There is nothing that we fear,
Bold and courageous we march,
Danger will never faze us,
We will sully the school's name never,
You know we belong together,
You and I forever and ever,
Onwards and upwards we march,
We'll shy from battle never,
We need our Lebensraum,
We'll take the Rhineland,
And the Sudetenland,
Ein Volk, Ein Reich, Ein Rock.
Castlerock above all others,
Castlerock above all others.

If we'd played the game there and then, roysh, we'd have scored, like, 200 points or something. Every time I think about it, the hairs on the back of my, like, neck stand on end. I'm actually still thinking about it when Simon tells us it's time to kick ass and we stand up to go. Christian grabs me by the shoulders, roysh, and he's like, "YOU THE MAN, ROSS! YOU THE MAN!"

We walk out, roysh, and the noise is, like, deafening. Our goys are, like, totally drowning out Bartholomew's. We are talking totally. They're like, "WE ARE ROCK, WE ARE ROCK, WE ARE ROCK."

Then they're, like, ripping the piss by going, "WE'RE RICH AND WE KNOW WE ARE, WE'RE RICH AND WE KNOW WE ARE."

I just try to focus, roysh, practicing my kicking from, like, different angles, and everytime I score, our goys are like, "WE'VE GOT ROSS O'CARROLL-KELLY ON OUR TEAM, WE'VE GOT THE BEST TEAM IN THE LAND."

JP comes up to me, roysh, looking totally pissed off about something, and he's like, "Have you seen who their captain is?"

I'm like, "No."

He's like, "We're talking Jamie O'Connell-Keaveney" and he, like, points him out, roysh.

I walk over to him, and he's in a huddle with a couple of other goys, roysh, and they're trying to, like, psyche themselves up. I walk up to him and I'm like, "Jamie O'Connell-Keaveney?"

He's like, "Yeah."

I'm like, "You're history, man."

He's like, "Oh yeah, Sorcha said you were a spa."

I'm like, "That's it, you focking retard. You are totalled. You are focking TOTALLY totalled."

Simon has to drag me away, roysh, and he's like, "Come on, save it for the game, Ross."

That's exactly what I do. I settle my nerves by kicking a penalty after, like, three minutes. There's only quarter of an hour gone, roysh, and we're, like, 22-0 up. Then we, like, piss all over them totally. My kicking is SO good, we're talking five conversions and five penalties, and we win, like, 60-15.

Halfway through the second half, roysh, Jamie O'Connell-Keaveney, the toal spa, scores a penalty, roysh, and I'm, like, "Happy birthday to you," and he, like, pushes me, roysh. I'm like, "Do you want to finish this now?" and I'm about to deck him when the goys drag me away, roysh, and they're like, "Come on, Ross, you've already shown that retard who's boss."

The final whistle blows, roysh, and we're like, "YYY-

EEESSS!!!", all hugging each other and shit. Simon comes over and, like congratulates me and tells me my kicking was what gave everyone the confidence to play well. All the goys comes over and high-five me.

We're all walking off the pitch, roysh, and I spot Christian talking to this bunch of Mounties, who are, like, total babes. They're all wearing their school uniforms, except for Christian's girlfriend, Amie, who's like wearing one of his rugby shirts, blue O'Neill's tracksuit bottoms and Nike runners. I already know Amie to see, roysh, but Christian introduces me to the others and it's, like, Keeva, Jenny and Sarah Jane. Keeva's is a total babe, and we're talking total here. She looks like Angel from *Home and Away*.

She turns to me, roysh, and she's like, "Oh well done, you had a really great match."

I'm like, "Thanks."

Then Jenny's like, "Do you remember me?"

I'm like, "What?"

She's like, "Do you remember me?"

I'm like, "No, where do I know you from?"

She's like, "HELLO? I was on the Irish debating team last year. We were at a debate in your school."

I go, "Oh yeah, your speech was amazing." I didn't have a clue who she was, roysh, but she was, like, a total babe.

I'm like, "Are you going to the boozer?"

And she's like, "Totally. But we have to go to Eddie Rockets first. Change out of our uniforms."

I'm like, "I'll see you later then."

I'm walking into the dressing-room and someone calls my name, roysh, and I turn around and it's, like, the old man. He looks a total spa as usual in that focking sheepskin coat and that hat, and he's, like, smoking a cigar. What a TOTAL retard.

He's like, "Well done, Ross. You had a terrific game."

I'm like, "Yeah, yeah, yeah, give me some money."

He, like, takes out his wallet, roysh, and pulls out two £20 notes, which he hands to me and he's like, "Don't get too drunk now, Ross."

I'm like, "Yeh roysh! I'm HORLDY likely to on forty focking quid now, am I?"

He storts to walk away, roysh, and I'm like, "And do you have to wear that focking hat?" but he totally blanks me.

I get back to the dressing-room, roysh, and the goys are all, like, crowding around, giving someone a wedgy. I ask JP who it is and he says it's Fionn, who had to face kangaroo court for, like, dropping the ball when he could have, like, set Simon up for a try. I grab my mobile and go into on of the traps to check my messages.

There are two, both from last night. Sorcha says she's SO embarrassed about the way she behaved in Annabel's and that I must think she is SUCH a knacker but even though she knows it's over she still has feelings for me and hopes we can be friends and we need to talk maybe over a drink. Then she says good luck in the match.

The second message was from Sian who's wondering why I haven't phoned her, obviously can't take the focking hint. She's SO totally trying to play it cool and she says she presumes I must have lost her number and she, like, gives it to me again, TOTALLY sad bitch, and she wishes me luck in the game and tells me I deserve it to go well because I've worked so hard.

All of a sudden someone's banging on the door, roysh, and it's Gicker and he's like, "Who's in trap one?"

I'm like, "It's me. Ross."

Then, roysh, Fionn's jocks come flying over the top of the door and land on my head. I pull them off, open the door and, like, run out totally freaking. All the goys are, like, cracking up, roysh, and then I stort laughing and I high-five JP, Simon, Terry and Newer. Fionn is lying on the ground with, like, blood gushing from his nose. Then all the goys burst into a round of, "I will if you do so will I."

Christian comes over to me, roysh, and he tells me that Keeva is totally mad about me, and that she's Amie's best friend and she, like, lives in Donnybrook and her old man is a doctor and she's totally loaded. I tell him that's cool, roysh, and I get changed. I'm wearing a blue broadcloth button down shirt from Tommy Hilfiger, straight pleated khakis from Gap, brown Dubarry Docksiders and a grey sleeveless bubble jacket, also from Gap.

We head into the boozer and the girls are already there. Keeva is wearing a baby blue short-sleeved top by Kookai, dark blue Diesel jeans and black boots by Red or Dead. Amie is wearing a light pink, short-sleeved top by Warehouse, a black wool shrug by Alberta Ferretti, black 501s and boots by Elle. Jenny is wearing a white belly-top by Morgan, black hipster trousers from French Connection and black Buffalo runners. Sarah Jane is wearing a blue and white striped rugby shirt from Benetton with the collar up, ice blue 501s and brown Dubarry Docksiders. She keeps saying that she feels like SUCH a total knacker.

Keeva gets me a pint and we stort chatting. She tells me I played really well and I'm like, "Thanks." Then she launches into this whole, like, school is such a total pain thing, roysh. She tells me her parents are, like, giving her LOADS of hassle about studying at the moment, and she's applying for International Commerce with French in UCD, but she's going to have to get her finger out and stort studying her orse off because she hasn't done a tap all year. I'm knocking back the pints at this stage, roysh. She tells me she's also deputy head girl and she also plays the piano and she's been asked to, like, arrange the music for the graduation and she still doesn't know what song they're going to do, roysh, but it's either *Never Forget* by Take That, *Hero* by Mariah Carey, or *You Are The Wind Beneath My Wings* by Bette Midler, which is, like, her favourite song of all time.

She asks me which one I'd choose and I tell her *Hero* and she asks why and I tell her because I like love songs.

She's like, "Yeah, rosyh. DON'T tell me you're romantic."

I'm like, "I am romantic."

She's like, "Yeah, roysh."

I turn around to Christian, roysh, and I'm lke, "Christian, aren't I romantic" but he's totally locked already, roysh.

He's like, "What?" He can hordly see in front of him and he has, like, a moustache of Guinness froth on his top lip, which he hasn't even had the cop-on to wipe off.

He's like, "What did you say?"

I'm like, "Forget it."

I order another pint and, like, ask Keeva if she wants another vodka and diet 7-Up, but she says she's cool. I take a sip out of my pint and I'm like, "No, I really am a romantic."

She goes, "Oh my God, you wouldn't have struck me as that type."

I go, "Yeah. I fall in love too easily, that's my biggest problem." Then I'm like, "Can I kiss you?"

And she goes, "Yeah." I end up being with her, roysh, and she's a totally amazing shift, but then about 20 minutes later I remember the porty in Simon's gaff, and I'm like, "Oh my God, what time is it?"

She looks at her watch, roysh, which is, like, a light blue Baby-G. She goes, "Nine o'clock."

I'm like, "Oh MY God, we're going to be late for the porty."

She's like, "Where's the porty?"

I'm like, "Simon's gaff. But it's team only."

I turn around, roysh, and Terry is kissing Sarah Jane, and Newer is with Jenny, and I'm like, "We better go. The rest of the goys will have an eppo."

We go outside, roysh, hail down a Jo Maxi and head up to Simon's gaff on Ailesbury Road. Totally amazing house. We're talking totally here. His old pair are in New York for a long weekend.

Simon opens the door, roysh, and he's like, "Where the fock have you been?"

I'm like, "Sorry, we were with these TOTAL babes."

He's like, "Those Mounties I saw you talking to?"

Newer goes, "Yeah."

Simon's like, "It's true what they say, they always get their man."

I high-five him, roysh, and we go in and all the rest of the goys are there.

Fionn's like, "Glad you could make it, goys. Beer's in the kitchen."

I grab a can of Heino, roysh, and sit down on the floor in the sitting-room with my back to the wall. We have SUCH a laugh. All the goys are, like, totally locked, roysh, and then we move onto spirits, vodka and Red Bull, and flaming Sambuccas.

The games begin at around midnight. First it's, like, Chariots of Fire. Everyone is given a long strip of, like, toilet paper, roysh, and they have to shove one end up their orse and, like, light the other end. The last one to pull theirs out is the winner. Then there's, like, Mince Pies, roysh, which is where everyone puts, like, a mince pie between the cheeks of their orse and then they all have to race to the end of the gorden, touch the wall and come back without dropping it. Then you have to squat over your pint and drop the pie in without touching it. The last one to do it has to, like, eat all the other mince pies.

I lose one game of that and three games of Soggy Biscuit, which

I find, like, impossible to play with drink on me, and I wake up on the floor in, like, Simon's room. I'm still wearing my clothes and I've vommed all over the place. We are talking ALL over the place. I can just about make out the figures of, like, Fionn and JP on the floor beside me. Simon's in the total horrors.

He's like, "Are you goys still alive?"

I'm like, "I don't think so."

He goes, "We'd better get up. Double chemistry in half an hour."

I haven't even got the strength to say, 'Yeah, roysh."

2
• • •

THE doorbell has been ringing for the last, like, 20 minutes, roysh, and I've been screaming for someone to answer it, but no-one has, so I presume the old pair have gone into town. I look at my alarm clock and it's, like, half ten, roysh, and I'm like, 'Who the fock is calling to the door at this time on a Saturday morning?'

I go downstairs to answer it wearing a grey Russell Athletic t-shirt and boxer shorts by Calvin Klein and it's, like, Sorcha. I'm about to ask her what the fock she wants, roysh, when she hands me a large bottle of cK One and goes, "peace offering".

I'm, like, freezing my orse off standing at the door in my boxers, roysh, so I have to ask her in.

It's only when we get into the kichen that I notice how amazing she looks. We're talking totally here, roysh. She's wearing a charcoal grey cashmere polo neck by Calvin Klein, grey woolen boot cut trousers by Donna Karan and black boots by Dolce & Gabbana. She's not wearing a coat, even though it's, like, freezing outside, but she has, like, a pink scorf and pink gloves, and she's also wearing a pair of Chloe aviator sunglasses, but as a hair band. Her perfume is Issey Miyake. I SO want to be with her, but I play it totally cool, roysh.

I'm like, "You're up early this morning."

She goes, "I'm going into town. I wondered if you wanted to come with me."

I'm like, "What for?"

She's like, "The January sales. Dad gave me £300."

29

I go, "Aren't the sales over yet?"

She's like, "HELLO? Get with the programme, Ross. The BT2 sale is only STORTING today."

I'm like, "Do you want coffee?"

She goes, "Yeah, but I'll make it while you get dressed."

I open the cupboard, roysh, and I'm, like, rooting around, trying to find where the old dear keeps that gourmet stuff she buys. Sorcha comes over and, like, crouches down beside me, and I'm like, 'Oh my God, I'm going to have to hop her'. That Issey Miyake is, like, SUCH a turn-on. We're talking totally here.

She's like, "I saw what Tony Ward wrote about you. Were you pleased?"

I'm like, "Yeah. We've still a long way to go until the final though". I pull out a packet of Jaffa Cakes.

She goes, "You're not going to get, like, totally big-headed now, are you?"

I'm like, "No. Where the fock does she keep the coffee?"

Sorcha's like, "You are TOTALLY blind" and she reaches into the cupboard and pulls out, like, a little green bag from Gloria Jean's, which she examines closely, and she goes, "Oh my God, French vanilla! I TOTALLY love French vanilla!"

She asks me where the old dear keeps the plunger and then tells me to go and get dressed. I go upstairs and put on a light blue Oxford shirt by French Connection, black baggy jeans by DKNY, brown Docksiders from Dubarry and a glacier blue lambswool v-neck from Gap, which I tie around my waist. I also wear a black Ralph Lauren baseball cap and aftershave by Carolina Herrera. I go back downstairs, roysh, and Sorcha has the coffee ready. She's standing next to the sink. She still has her gloves on and she's, like, holding her mug with both hands and she, like, blows into her coffee before taking tiny sip.

I'm like, "So what are you going to buy today?"

She doesn't answer, roysh, just keeps smiling at me, which is, like, totally wrecking my head, and eventually I'm like, "What?"

Sorcha's like, "Who's Alyson?"

I'm like, "What?"

She's like, "Who's Alyson?"

I go, "I don't know what you're talking about."

She goes, "Your mother left you a note on the table to say Alyson phoned last night." She doesn't sound pissed off or anything, she's just, like, totally ripping the piss out of me.

I'm like, "She's just a friend." Sorcha laughs.

She's like, "I'm not jealous, Ross."

I'm like, "Good."

She goes, "Look, Ross, I've been doing a lot of thinking. I was totally out of order in Annabel's. I accept that. Maybe I underestimated the way I felt. I thought I was, like, TOTALLY over you, but when I saw you with Sian Kennedy, I just totally flipped. I thought at first it was because she's SUCH a knob, but then I realised that I still have strong feelings for you."

I interrupt her, roysh, and tell her it sounds like it's getting too heavy, but she's like, "Let me finish, Ross. I do still have strong feelings for you. I can't deny that. But I accept that it's over between us. And I guess what I'm trying to say is that I value your friendship too much to ever want to lose you."

We're talking, 'Oh my God, let me the fock out of here'.

Sorcha's driving the RAV4 her old man bought her last year for her nineteenth. She has the new Robbie Williams album in the cor, roysh, and she, like, totally loses it when *Angels* comes on. She's like, "Oh my God. Oh my God. This is my favourite song of, like, ALL time." When it's over, she asks me to rewind it again, roysh, and we listen to it for the second time and then she tells me that it reminds her of Josh, this goy she met in the PoD a few weeks ago.

I feel a bit, like, jealous, roysh, but I know her game, and I just agree that it's a totally amazing song and I rewind it and play it again, which must totally wreck her head. I spend the rest of the time flipping through a magazine which was, like, on my seat when I got in. There's an article in it about dieting with the headline: "WHAT YOU EAT TODAY, YOU WEAR TOMORROW."

We pork in the Stephen's Green Shopping Centre, roysh, and Sorcha, like, drags me in to Benetton to see if Emma's working. They're both in first year Orts UCD, roysh, and Emma is a total babe. And we are talking total here. She looks like Cameron Diaz. She's wearing a fuchsia shirt from Benetton, grey wide-leg wool-mix trousers by French Connection and black ponyskin slingbacks by, I think, Dolce & Gabbana. Emma tells Sorcha that she missed her 11 o'clock again on Thursday and Sorcha says that she went to her Tuesday two o'clock for the first time ever last week and the lecturer practically asked her for ID.

Emma reminds Sorcha that she still has, like, notes belonging to her and they arrange to meet in Hilper's on Wednesday afternoon. Sorcha asks Emma what she's doing tonight but Emma doesn't know, and neither does Sorcha, and they exchange names of a couple of nightclubs they might end up going to. Then they stort talking about goys they're in college with and I'm, like, totally bored, and Sorcha decides it's time to go when I stort, like, unfolding clothes, and they airkiss each other goodbye and say they'll meet on Wednesday. We get outside the shop and Sorcha says that Emma is a total knob and a sly bitch and she wouldn't trust her as far as she could throw her.

She links my arm as we walk down Grafton Street and steers me into BT2. The next, like, hour is a total mare. The shop is FULL of skangers. We are talking major here. These two slappers are giving Sorcha, like, total filthies.

I'm like, "Sorry, do you have a problem?"

And one of them's like, "Fuck off, ye fuckin poshie."

I'm like, "Fock off back to Pram Springs, you total slapper."

I turn to Sorcha and I'm like, "This place is total focking Knackeragua."

Sorcha's like, "What do they expect? They are offering, like, 70% off clothes. It's bound to attract those kinds of people."

I'm like, "I know what you mean. It's like TK Maxx. Every skanger in Dublin is wearing Ralph Lauren since they opened."

Sorcha buys a blue fitted jacket by Dolce & Gabbana, black knee length boots by Alberta Ferretti, a black hooded evening dress by Elle Active and two white sleeveless t-shirts by French Connection. She pays for them with her gold card.

We go and look at the men's clothes then and I, like, cannot believe it. The black and white RL sweater I bought before Christmas is reduced from £110 to £55. The blue and white striped Polo Sport rugby shirt the old pair got me for Christmas is reduced from £115 to, like, £80.

I turn to Sorcha and I'm like, "This is totally unfair. I've a good mind to ask for the focking manager."

Sorcha goes, "Cheer up, I bought you this," and she hands me this bag, roysh, and I'm like, "What is it?", and she's like, "Open it."

I open it, roysh, and it's, like, a white Armani Jeans baseball cap, with, like, a black AJ insignia on the front. I take off my Ralph Lauren baseball cap and put it on. Sorcha says it SO suits me. She's like, "You already have a black one, don't you?"

I'm like, "No."

She's like, "I thought I saw you wearing it in the Red Box two Saturdays ago."

I'm like, "No. Maybe that was Josh."

She just, like, smiles at that and then she's like, "Anyway, I bought that for you to say thanks for coming into town with me."

I'm like, "Thanks".

Then she's like, "Come on, I'll treat you to a cappuccino."

We're about to go into Café Java, roysh, and who do we meet – TOTAL shamer – only the old pair. I'm there going, 'Oh my God, this is not happening'. They've been shopping, roysh, and they're, like, holding hands, pass the focking sick bag. I pretend not to see them at first, roysh, but Sorcha, the total spa, is like, "Oh my God, Ross, it's your mum and dad", and she goes over, roysh. The old dear makes a total meal of saying hello, airkissing her in front of half of focking South Anne Street.

I'm there going, 'Okay, get me OUT of here'. The old man has obviously cracked open the wallet, because the old dear has, like, a bag from Pia Bang and a smile on her face which goes from focking ear to ear. The old man is carrying a bag from, like, Marks and Spencers. Sorcha is, like, totally licking the old dear's orse.

She's like, "Oh my God, you look so well." Then she says she hopes she doesn't mind but she had some of her Gloria Jeans this morning and, like, the old dear says that's fine and mentions that they've just come out of Marks and Spencers, roysh, and I have to listen to them prattle on for focking ten minutes about how amazing their food is.

The old dear is there going, "Have you tried their fennel bread?"

And Sorcha's like, "It's amazing, isn't it? I love their dips" and then she's like, "totally fattening though".

The old dear tells Sorcha that she doesn't have to worry about her figure and then the old man gets in on the act, roysh.

He's there going, "Did you see what Tony Ward wrote about Ross?"

Sorcha's like, "I did. You must be SO proud."

The old man's like, "Well, Tony Ward recognises that he's a future international. When is Gerry Thornley going to wake up, that's what I want to ask."

Then the old dear, roysh, she asks whether we want to join them in the Westbury for afternoon tea and Sorcha's goes "Yeah", and I'm like, "AS IF!" I stort to drag Sorcha away and the old man, what a TOTAL retard, is like, "It's great to see the two of you together again."

I'm like, 'HELLO?'

We get a table near the window in Café Java. Sorcha takes off her gloves and her scorf and, like, lays them down on the table before looking at the menu. She orders a feta cheese salad with tomato bread and no olives, a ham and camembert croissant and a Diet Coke. I order a club sandwich, which comes with, like, a side order of Pringles, and a Coke, but I'm still storving afterwards, so I also order, like, a ciabatta filler, and then a chocolate concorde.

Sorcha says she has been eating SO much shit in college all week and she doesn't want dessert, but she ends up eating half of mine. I order a coffee and she has, like, an espresso mallowchino, which she plays with for, like, ten minutes, with her spoon, making different shapes out of the marshmallow as it melts on the surface. I can, like, tell there's something on her mind.

Eventually, she, like, puts her spoon down, takes off her scrunchy and slips it onto her wrist, shakes her head, pulls all of her hair back into a low ponytail again, puts the scrunchy back on and then pulls five or six strands of hair forward.

Then she's like, "Ross, I have something to ask you?"

I'm like, "What?"

She's like, "Okay, I'm going to come straight out with it. Will you come to the Orts Ball with me. Just as a friend."

I'm like, "Why don't you ask lover boy?"

She goes, "Who?"

I'm like, "Jamie what's-his-name?"

She's like, "Jamie is a dickhead."

I go, "But you said –"

And she's like, "HELLO? I know what I said, Ross. I was wrong. Please will you come with me. I'd really like you to be there." I fiddle with her cigarette lighter for a few seconds and then I'm like, "Roysh, I'll go, but just as friends." I am DYING to be with her now, but I don't want to, like, get into that whole focking going out together shit again.

Sorcha takes out a packet of Marlboro Lights and I go into the jacks, have a slash, wash my hands, splash water on my face and then take out the mobile. There are four new messages. Keeva phoned and said she is SO embarrassed and she has never done anything like this before but she got my number from, like, Christian and she's probably making a TOTAL spa of herself but she really enjoyed that night and she isn't really doing anything for, like, the weekend and she wondered whether I wanted to go out to her house down in, like, Delgany, and watch MTV or maybe, like, go for a drink or for something to eat or the cinema or whatever. She leaves her number and asks me to phone her back but not on Saturday morning because she has, like, horseriding.

The next two messages are hang-ups, but I can see that they've both come from Sian's mobile number, one at half-eleven last night and the other at five past ten this morning. The fourth call is from a girl called Claire, who says she is Sian's best friend and she tells me I'm a TOTAL asshole because of the way I treated her and I should pray that I don't ever run into her because if there's one thing she prides herself on it's being a good friend and she doesn't know why Sian is constantly falling for dickheads like me. Then she screams DICKHEAD down the phone four times and tells me that any girl who has ever been with me says that I have a small penis. I snap the phone shut, check myself out in the mirror again and return to the table, where Sorcha is handing the waitress her cord and asking for a glass of Ballygowan, still. Something's wrong. She is being FAR too nice.

* * * *

SIMON HAS A VERY HAIRY BODY, DOESN'T HE? I hear these words from, like, underneath my towel as I'm drying my hair, roysh, and at first I'm not sure whose voice it is or whether I've, like, mis-heard it, but when I take the towel away I discover that it's Eunan, who's, like, a boarder, and a total focking weirdo, and then he says it again and I ask him what he means and he's like, "Just that. He has a very hairy body."

I am NOT getting in the shower while he's in the dressing-room. He was being, like, totally weird after the game, and we are talking TOTAL here. We pissed all over Thaddeus' Community School, roysh – a skanger school, NORTHSIDERS for fock's sake – and after the game I was walking around, like, searching out our goys to say well done and we were all, like celebrating, and every time I turned around he was there, giving me, like, a hug, roysh. And he was doing it, like, FAR too enthusiastically for my liking.

I'm there going, "HELLO? This is NOT normal." He SO should face kangaroo court for this and we are talking totally here.

Thaddeus' were a total pushover and I have, like, never met such a bunch of focking knackers in my life. All through the game, their fans are like, "DADDY'S GOING TO BUY YOU A BRAND NEW MOTORCAR" and our goys are, like, "YOU'RE FROM SKANGER-VILLE, YOU'RE FROM SKANGER-VILLE." We run in, like, ten tries and I kick, like, seven conversions and six penalties, and we win 82-6. We are talking TOTAL pushovers here.

Anyway, roysh, I don't chance having a shower, roysh. I just, like, wash my face and under my arms while Eunan stares me out of it. I throw on my clothes – we're talking blue and white cheque shirt by Dockers, baggy petrol blue jeans by Armani and brown boots by Timberland – and go outside. I see Sorcha's friend, Aoife, talking to Fionn, who she's been, like, seeing since she broke up with Cian, our prop forward two weeks ago. She looks really well, a bit on the thin side, but she's, like, actually a stunner and she looks like Natalie Imbruglia except with long hair. She's drinking a bottle of Evian, and she's wearing a royal blue fitted shirt by French Connection with the collar up, navy combats by Hobo and black Buffalo run-ners. She also has, like, a Castlerock rugby shirt tied around her waist. She introduces us to Ciara, who's, like, in her class in ATIM, and she's alright looking, a bit like Libby from *Neighbours*. She's wearing a white hooded fleece with Susst on the front, blue O'Neills tracksuit bottoms and brown Pepe docksiders. Ciara tells me that they both took the afternoon off college to go the game and they were supposed to have accountancy but it's, like, TOTALLY boring although college is alright and the social life is amazing, but neither her nor Aoife has done a tap all year and they're going to have to SERIOUSLY pull their socks up.

I'm only, like, half listening to this, roysh, because I notice two girls who are standing around, like, waiting to talk to me. Even though they're not wearing their uniforms, I know for definite that they are Whores on the Shore, because I've seen them around. Ciara, who's obviously a total spa, is still in mid sentence when I walk away and go over to them.

I'm like, "Hi."

They're both like, "Hi-how-or-ya?"

I'm like, "Cool."

The best looking of the two makes the introductions. Her name is, like, Joanna, and she is a total ringer for Chloe out of *Home and Away*, and her friend, who's alright looking, is Keelin. Joanna is wearing a white long sleeved t-shirt by Morgan, black Calvin Klein jeans, black penny loafers by, I think, Next, and a grey duffel jacket by Dolce & Gabbana. Keelin is wearing a pink Lacoste shirt with the collar up, ice blue 501s, black penny loafers by Bally and a black sleeveless bubble jacket by Polo Sport. I tell them my name and they say they already know, roysh, and Keelin tells me that I know her cousin really well, and I ask her what her cousin's name is and she says it's Cara Hanley.

I'm like, "The name's familiar."

And she goes, "She knows you from Irish college last summer."

I haven't a clue who she's talking about, but I pretend I do and agree with her when she says Cara's, like, totally cool and a really nice person and one of the few people you could actually call a true friend.

We're standing there chatting away, roysh, when this goy comes over. I recognise him straight away. He's, like, one of the backs off the other team. He has one eye closed, roysh, and he comes up to me and, like, offers me his hand and he's like, "Put it there, bud."

I don't know if he's ripping the piss or what, roysh, but I shake his hand and then, like, ask him what happened to his eye.

He's like, "It was poked out by your girlfriend's collar." Then he just, like, bursts out laughing, roysh, and walks over to this, like, other bunch of skangers, who are, like, breaking their shites laughing as well, and he tells them that he said it.

Joanna shakes her head and she's like, "I don't know why they even let schools like that in the competition. They can't even play the sport."

Keelin goes, "That's the first time I've ever seen a real sovereign ring. Oh sure, I've seen them on television and in photographs, but never in real life."

I ask the girls whether they're, like, heading to the boozer and they say they are, roysh, and we wait for the rest of the goys and we all, like, head up together. Fionn has a big mork on his cheek were some skanger bit him in the scrum and Christian shows us the stud morks on his shoulder where he got stamped. Keelin shakes her hand and says, "total skangers."

All the girls stort introducing themselves to one another then, roysh, and we head into the boozer. Everyone's buying me drink and at one stage I've got, like, six pints in front of me and I'm knocking them back, roysh, and I'm, like, totally locked out of my tree. I'm so locked in fact that I don't even notice that Joanna and Keelin have, like, gone home, got changed and come back again, because Joanna is now wearing a white Scott Henshall shirt, black parallel trousers by Amanda Wakeley and boots by Carl Scarpa, and Keelin is wearing a navy slash neck top by, I think, Morgan, dark blue Armani jeans and boots by Guess, which I presume means we're all, like, heading on somewhere after.

We end in up a nightclub that looks familiar but I'm, like, too shit-faced to recognise which one it is and the next thing I remember is, like, Joanna and Keelin dragging me out onto the dancefloor for some Backstreet Boys song, I think it's *Backstreet's Back*, and I can hordly stand I'm so locked. But then *I Believe I Can Fly* comes on and, like, Joanna holds me up while we're slow-dancing, and then it's *Two Become One* by the Spice Girls, which Joanna says she SO loves. I snog her on the dancefloor, roysh, and she is a totally amazing shift, but the night is a total bummer from then on. Maybe it's the drink, but I'm on a bit of a downer.

Aoife and Fionn are having, like, a major fight and we are talking MAJOR here. She's, like, totally hysterical and I can't make out a word she's saying, but Fionn is trying to hug her and he's like, "Don't be stupid, Aoife, you ARE pretty."

Simon comes over to me, roysh, and I'm so locked I can't even focus properly, and he's like, "Are you thinking of entering Kruffs this year."

I'm like, "What?"

He goes, "I'm just wondering what the fock you're doing with that total mutt?" and he points to Joanna, who's, like, back on the dancefloor, roysh.

I'm like, "She's not a mutt."

And Cian, who's, like, standing beside him, roysh, he goes, "I have to say, I think she's alright from a distance."

And Simon's like, "Yeah, Dublin to focking New York. At night." Which I know is, like, total bullshit, because Simon tried to be with her ages ago and he totally crashed and burned. I remind him of this and he just, like, smiles and high-fives me and then focks off.

Anyway, roysh, the night totally flies by and next thing I know, all the other goys are gone and it's only me, Christian, Joanna and Keelin left. Christian appears to be with Keelin, as in *with* with. I wonder whether he's still going out with Amie, though that's a totally stupid question because he's always, like, doing the dirt, and he must be able to read my mind, roysh, because he puts his arm around my shoulder and whispers in my ear, "An erect micky has no conscience", which is, like, his favourite phrase. The four of us end up staying in Keelin's house in Monkstown. Her parents are in London for the week and she has, like, a free gaff.

The next morning, roysh, I wake up early and my head is hopping. I'm there going, 'Oh my God, I want to die.' We are talking totally here. I try to get dressed without waking Joanna but she hears me as I'm, like, putting on my shoes and she asks me where I'm going. I tell her I have to go home or the old dear will have an eppo. She tells me she had a really nice time last night and not to worry about you-know-what and do I think we should see each other again and I'm like, "whatever."

She asks for my number and I'm tempted to give her a false one but I'm, like, too hungover to make one up, so I give it to her and she writes it with an eyebrow pencil on the cover of the new *Image*. She tells me that there's a photograph of one of her best friends in it and she storts flicking through the pages, but I tell her I have to go and she says okay and blows me a kiss as I'm leaving and I just, like, smile at her.

I have two messages. I don't know who the first one is from but I can, like, take a guess, because that song *Short Dick Man* is on in the background and someone is holding the phone up to the speaker. The second message is from Keeva, who wants to know why I stood her up in Blackrock on Friday night, why I haven't returned any of her calls since then and why I'm doing a total Chandler on her. I get the Dort to Dun Laoghaire, buy *The Irish Times* and the *Irish Independent* at the train station and I, like, read the reports on yesterday's game while I wait for the bus.

Tony Ward wrote, like, half a page on the match and it was like, "The schools game is the bedrock of rugby in this country and MAKE NO MISTAKE ABOUT IT the performance by Castlerock in the second round of the schools cup yesterday was as fine an exhibition of how the game should be played as you are likely to see at any level. This team is simply awesome and the game was a particular tour de force for young Ross O'Carroll-Kelly, who is an undoubted star for the future."

The Irish Times only carried, like, six paragraphs on the game, but not by Gerry Thornley, who's apparently covering Five Nations stuff at the moment, roysh, so the report was written by some freelance, who described my kicking as "unerring", whatever the fock that means.

I get home, roysh, and the old dear doesn't even mention the fact that I didn't come home last night. She's sitting in dad's study, roysh, and she's wearing her glasses, which means that she's probably writing letters to all the local councillors again about this halting site they're planning to build down the road. I walk past the study and she shouts out to me, "You'll have to fix your own breakfast, Ross. I have to prepare for tonight's committee meeting."

I'm like, "You mean Fockrock Against Total Skangers?"

She's like, "That is not the name of it, Ross, as well you know."

I'm like, "I don't really care what your anti-halting site group is called."

She goes, "We're not anti-halting site, Ross. We just happen to feel that it wouldn't be appropriate for this area."

I go, "Whatever", and go into the kitchen to get some breakfast.

* * * *

WHAT'S big, brown and ugly and hangs off the side of a satellite dish? The answer is a council house and I've already heard it before, but I couldn't be orsed telling Kenny, this total RETARD who Sorcha has insisted we share a table with, and anyway I can't get my mind or my eyes off Amanda, this TOTAL ride who's apparently in second Orts. Sorcha notices this.

She's like, "Ross, your chicken is going cold" but I totally blank here and keep staring. All week long, I've been listening to Sorcha and all her friends going on about Amanda Cooper and how she was wearing the famous Liz Hurley dress to the Orts Ball, the black Versace one with the gold safety pins, which cost, like, 80 lids each or something. Now I know why they were so worried, roysh, because there isn't a goy in the place who can keep his eyes off her, and that's saying something considering the talent that's here.

Sorcha looks totally amazing herself. She's wearing a blue felt, backless ballgown by Amanda Wakeley and blue slingbacks by Patrick Cox. She also has, like, a Louis Vuitton Pakatoa bag, which her old dear brought her back from the States last Christmas, and her perfume is Freedom by Tommy Hilfiger. Her friend Ruth, who is, like, the image of Gwyneth Paltrow – I was with her, like, during the summer, although Sorcha doesn't know – she looks totally amazing in a black halter neck dress from Chanel and black slingbacks from Red or Dead. Aisling, this total babe who for some strange reason, seems to be going out with Kenny, is wearing a pink crushed velvet dress by Ralph Lauren and black sandles by Prada. I'm wearing a Ralph Lauren tuxedo, which I had to, like, borrow from JP's older brother, Greg, and a novelty shirt which is, like, white, roysh, but has cartoon characters on the sleeves. Sorcha has a total knicker-fit when I, like, take off my jacket at the table.

She's there going, "Oh my God, I am SO embarrassed."

Oisínn, who has come with Rebecca, who's, like, a friend of his sister, he's wearing one as well, but he's, like, sitting at a different table.

The skivvies come to collect the plates, and I notice that none of the girls at our table have, like, touched their food. Our skivvy is, like, muttering under her breath, roysh, and Ruth is like, "Sorry, have you got a problem?"

The skivvy's like, "I just said it's a terrible waste of food."

Ruth goes, "So?"

And the skivvy's like, "So, you cheeky little madam, there's young children starving in Africa."

And Kenny goes, "I doubt if they'd eat chicken supreme". Which is, like, the only decent thing he's said all night. Your one says we're a bunch of spoilt brats, roysh, and Sorcha's like, "Sorry, excuse me. My father is Edmund Lalor. From Edmund Lalor and Portners? He has all of his conferences in this hotel. He spends a FORTUNE here. Now, if you want to keep your job, I'd advise you to fock off and leave us alone."

And your one bursts into tears, roysh, and focks off. Sorcha, like, stares at her as she leave, while at the same time pulling out a Marlboro Light. Then Sorcha, Ruth and Aisling stort bitching about other girls in their year, especially some girl called Sarah who's wearing a yellow ballgown that Ruth says looks as though it's made out of tissue paper. Kenny, and this other spa who's at our table, try to get a bit of a conversation going and they ask me what club I'm signing for when I leave Castlerock, but I couldn't be orsed even answering them and I look around and there's, like, an actual food fight happening at Oisínn's table and his shirt is covered in chocolate. Totally covered. A new skivvy arrives at our table, roysh, and Sorcha says she doesn't want profiteroles and Ruth and Aisling say they don't either.

Aisling goes, "A moment on the lips, a lifetime on the hips," as she pulls on one of Sorcha's Marlboro Lights. Ruth says she wants coffee and Sorcha says it must be black. I'm eating my profiteroles, roysh, and Sorcha asks can she have just one, but ends up eating three, and Kenny is asking Aisling why the fock she didn't get her own and she's telling him she only wants one, but he, like, pushes the bowl at her and tells her to eat them all and stop making a spa of herself.

I am totally bored at this stage, roysh, and I'm, like, looking around, and I notice Amanda Cooper on her own up at the bor. I go up to her, roysh, and introduce myself, but she's, like, totally cold to me.

I go, "Your dress is amazing" and she, like, throws her eyes up the heaven. I ask can I get her a drink and she tells me she's with her boyfriend and I'm like, "I only want to buy you a drink."

She ignores this, roysh, and when the borman comes over she asks for a bottle of Coors Light.

I'm like, "I better lay off the sauce myself. I've a big game next Wednesday. I play rugby."

All of a sudden, roysh, I feel this tap on my shoulder and I turn around and there's this, like, total babe, and we are talking total here. She looks like Teri Hatcher from *Superman* and she's obviously a friend of Amanda. She's wearing a black strapless wool dress with boned bodice by Dolce & Gabbana and black sandals by Elle.

I introduce myself, roysh, and she's like, "I don't care who you are. What makes you think either of us would be interested in you?" and she, like, looks me up and down.

I go, "I'm just being friendly, that's all."

And she goes, "Yeah, fock off back to your little rugby groupies."

What a total shamer and we are talking total here. I walk back from the bor, roysh, and Oisínn calls me over and tells me he saw me talking to Amanda Cooper and, like, asks what she said. I shake my head and go, "lesbian". And he laughs and high-fives me. I sit talking to him for, like, an hour, roysh, and this girl comes over and sits beside me. She's a total dog and she's, like, focking huge, roysh.

She goes, "You're Ross, aren't you? You used to go out with Sorcha."

I tell her I did and she says her name is Georgia and she's one of Sorcha's best friends, although I've never heard Sorcha mention her before. She asks me what school I go to and I tell her Castlerock and she's like, "Oh my God, do you know Patrick Newe?"

I tell her I do, that he's on the senior rugby team with me, and she's like, "I used to go out with him when I was eight. Oh my God, I can't believe you know Patrick Newe. And do you know Gavin Doyle?" This girl is a total knob.

I'm like, "Yeah, I know Gavin Doyle."

She goes, "He's my next-door neighbour. Well, he lives about five doors away. Oh my God, I can't believe you know Gavin Doyle."

I am totally bored after, like, about ten minutes of this, so I head back to our table and on the way over, roysh, I notice that this goy is, like, hanging out of Sorcha.

I go over and sit down and Kenny has bought me a pint of Heino and I sit there for about ten minutes, talking to him about rugby and, like, trying to stay cool. But this goy is, like, ALL focking over her and eventually I'm like, "Sorcha, can I talk to you?"

The goy, who's, like, a total spa, roysh (he's got focking glasses and, like, a quiff) he's like, "What's your focking problem, man?"

I go, "You're sitting in my seat".

And he, like, points over to the jacks, roysh, and he's like, "your seat's in there, rugby boy".

I'm about to, like, deck him when Sorcha grabs me and drags me away, and she's like, "I'm really sorry, Paul".

And he's like, "It's okay. Give me a ring during the week, Sorcha."

And she's like, "I will."

She pushes me up as far as the bor, roysh, and she's like, "What is YOUR problem?"

I'm like, "Who's that focking spa?"

She's goes, "His name is Paul. He's in my class. He's a really good friend of mine."

It's only then that I notice how locked she is. She's a total wuss when it comes to drinking and she's only had, like, four bottles of Miller, but she's totally off her face.

She's like, "I asked you a question, Ross."

I'm like, "What?"

She's like, "I asked you what was your problem with me talking to Paul."

I shrug my shoulders and I'm like, "I was jealous, I suppose."

She's there going, "Ross, we're not going out together anymore. You dumped me, remember?"

I'm like, "You were the one who broke it off."

She goes, "HELLO? You kissed my best friend, Ross. I don't

THINK I was being unreasonable."

I'm like, "it was a mistake, Sorcha. I really miss you. Especially your friendship."

She's like, "bullshit". She's totally off her face.

I'm like, "It's not bullshit, Sorcha. Ever since we broke up, I've been thinking about you all the time."

She goes, "Oh yeah? And what about all that stuff you gave me last time about wanting your freedom and, like, not wanting to be chained down."

I'm like, "I underestimated my feelings for you."

I kiss her, roysh, and then some song by Eternal comes on, I think it's like, *Oh Baby I*, and Sorcha says she SO loves that song and we HAVE to dance to it, so then we're out the dancefloor, snogging away. Halfway through the next song, which is, like, *A Million Love Songs Later* by Take That, Sorcha's like, "let's go upstairs".

I'm like, "Where?"

She goes, "I've booked a room. In the hotel."

I'm there going, 'TOUCHDOWN'. I'm like, "Okay, Sorcha. If it's what you really want."

She's like, "It is but I'm warning you, Ross, you better not mess me around. I don't want you to tell me in the morning that you don't like commitment. I don't want you doing a Chandler on me again." I'm trying to remember whether it was Keeva or Sian who said that to me the other day as we leave the dancefloor. We go up in the lift and, as she pushes the cord in the door of the room, she turns around and she's like, "It's a copy, by the way."

I'm there going, "What are you talking about?"

She's like, "Amanda Cooper's dress. It's not a real Versace. Her aunt is a dressmaker."

3
• • •

AN inappropriate gesture is what *The Irish Times* said I made to the crowd during the match on Friday. An inappropriate gesture? I'm there going, 'HELLO? I gave them the FINGER.' And it wasn't, like, inappropriate either. The crowd were giving me, like, major stick throughout the game and we are talking MAJOR here. Temple Hill were, like, a lot tougher than we thought and for some reason I had a total mare with my kicking. Their supporters were giving me LOADS, and about five minutes from the end, I got the ball and ran, like, 40 yords to score a try. I threw the ball up in the air, roysh, ran over to their supporters behind the goal and gave them the finger, as in 'Hey, who's in the FOCKING semi-final now?'

Anyway, roysh, I got up on Saturday morning and the old man was on to *The Irish Times* and he was, like, giving out yords. He was there going, "Your representative said my son made an inappropriate gesture, but made no reference whatsoever to the level of provocation he was subjected to."

The goy on the other end of the phone was, like, obviously trying to argue back, but he was getting nowhere, roysh, because the old man was going, "It's quite evident from your coverage that you care nothing for the schools game. It strikes me that Tony Ward, from your main rivals, is the only rugby writer who appreciates the seriousness of it. I mean, where the hell was Gerry Thornley on Friday?" There was, like, a pause, roysh, and the old man totally exploded. He was like, "Well get him back from Paris. Who gives a damn about the Five Nations?" He finished off by reminding the goy how much money he spends on, like, advertising every year with the paper and slammed the phone down.

Anyway, roysh, the whole team has been given the day off school today because we're, like, totally wrecked after the last few weeks. The training has been, like, totally intense and we are talking TOTALLY here. We've been training before school, at lunchtime and then afterwards as well and we're all like, 'Oh my God, this can't go on'. Plus, roysh, Sooty has turned into a total focking Nazi. He makes us sing *Castlerock Above All Others* before and after each session and he's storted wearing, like, jodhpurs and knee-high boots. He goes around talking to himself and, like, listening to Tony Quinn tapes on a Walkman. His new nickname among the goys is Mad Dog.

Anyway, roysh, because we all have the morning off, we decided to, like, do something together, as a team, for morale, roysh, so we all met at the Dort station in Blackrock and we're, like, heading out to Greystones to watch the Irish team train. Christian has had an offer to, like, play for Greystones U-19s next season and he wants an excuse to go down and, like, check out the facilities. We're having, like, a TOTAL laugh. JP and Fionn are, like, down the other end of the carriage, sitting next to these three girls from Pill Hill, who are, like, totally gagging for them, but the goys are, like totally ripping the piss. We're all there, like, singing, roysh, "WE WILL, WE WILL, ROCK YOU, FOCK YOU, ANYWAY YOU WANT TO" and the goys are like waving down to us. Simon high-fives me and I high-five Oisín and Christian and Newer, and Gicker high-fives Terry and Eunan, and then Eunan grabs me and gives me a hug and he's screaming like, "YOU THE MAN, ROSS. YOU THE MAN".

And all the goys are like, "WE'VE GOT ROSS O'CARROLL KELLY ON OUR TEAM, WE'VE GOT THE BEST TEAM IN THE LAND!".

This old goy, roysh, who got on the train at Sandycove, he turns around, roysh, and he's like, "Excuse me, there are other people on this train. Would you mind keeping your voices down."

And Gicker's like, "Fock off back to Jurassic Pork" and Christian calls him and old fort, roysh, and the goy gets off at Dalkey and we're all there going, "YYYEEEAAAHHH".

But he goes up and, like, storts talking to the driver, the total retard, and when the train storts again, the driver is like, "I would like to remind everyone on the train that they are on public transport and ask them to show some respect for other commuters. Otherwise, this service will terminate at the next station and the Gardaí will be called." We all give a big cheer, roysh, and JP and Fionn come back down and high-five me, Simon and Oisínn, and Terry high-fives Newer and Gicker.

Anyway, roysh, we stop at Killiney and JP jumps up and he's like, "Hey, Ross, there's Sorcha". And I look over the other side of the platform and she's, like, standing there, obviously heading into town, with Aoife. She actually looks really well. She's wearing a beige v-neck top by G-Star, cobalt blue boot cut jeans by DKNY, black boots by Marco Moreo and a white sleeveless bubble jacket by DKNY. Aoife is wearing a pink Lacoste airtex with the collar up, ice blue 501s and penny loafers by Next, and she has, like, a lilac polo neck jumper by Jigsaw tied around her waist. Christian says it must be cold out this morning, because he thinks Aoife is wearing TWO jumpers around her waist. We all, like, totally crack up. Anyway, roysh, they don't notice us for ages. Sorcha takes off her scrunchy, shakes her head, smoothes her hair back into a low pony tail, puts the scrunchy back on and pulls four or five strands of hair forward. Aoife, who's been seeing Terry since she broke up with Fionn, is eating a bag of popcorn and is scanning the train to see who's looking at her. When she notices us she waves and, like, nudges Sorcha and I can see her mouth the words, "Oh my God, there's Ross", and Sorcha, who's putting on lip balm, squints and, when she recognises me, makes the shape of a phone with her hand and she's like, "Ring me", and she looks majorly pissed off.

I haven't returned any of her calls for the last, like, three weeks, and the goys are all like, "WHOAH, who's in the bad books, Ross?" and then, as the Dort storts moving again, they're like, "ONE ROSS O'CARROLL KELLY, THERE'S ONLY ONE ROSS O'CAR-ROLL KELLY."

There were six messages when I checked this morning. Joanna rang on Thursday to see how I was and to say she presumed I hadn't been in touch was because I was so, like, focused on Friday's game and she wished me good luck and said some shit about me being capable of doing anything I want to in life once I put my mind to it. Then she said she'd see me, like, on Tuesday afternoon, whatever the fock she means. The second and third calls were from Sorcha, who said she needed to speak to me about something and it was TOTAL-LY urgent. The fourth call was at ten o'clock on Saturday night and it was, like, someone playing *Short Dick Man* down the phone again. Alyson, surprise surprise, and Joanna, yet again, phoned on Sunday afternoon to say they'd seen *The Irish Times* and wondered if I was alright and if I needed someone to talk to, blah blah blah.

We get off the Dort in Bray, roysh, and we're waiting for the bus to Greystones, and this Virgin on the Rocks comes up to Fionn and she's like, "Fionn O'Súilleabháinn?"

And he's like, "Yeah".

She goes, "You've been telling people you were with me."

Fionn's like, "No I haven't."

She's like, "You have. You told Esmé McConville and Kate Murray you were with me in the rugby club two weeks ago."

Fionn's like, "Fock off, you silly little girl." And she, like, flips the total lid, calls him a retard and slaps him across the face, roysh. Then she, like, storms off and Fionn's just there laughing.

He's like, "She is TOTALLY gagging for me". One side of his face is still, like, totally red when we get on the bus.

* * * *

I'M, like, SO worried about my kicking, roysh, that I stay behind for an extra 20 minutes after lunch to, like practice on my own; just, like, kicking ball after ball over the bor from different angles. It means that I'm, like, 20 minutes late for, like, double history, roysh, and I go in and Mister Coffey is like, "You're late".

I'm like, "No shit, Sherlock," which he didn't hear, roysh, but everyone else did and they, like, totally burst their shites laughing.

He's like, "Do you have an explanation, boy. One you would like to share with me, not just your little cheerleaders in the back row down there?"

I just, like, shrug my shoulders and I go, "I was out practicing my kicking."

He's like, "And no doubt occupying your mind with more cere-bral matters too, such as the causes of the First World War. Yes?"

I'm like, "Sorry?"

And he goes, "You were to have learned this off for today. What were the causes of the First World War?"

I'm like, "You don't understand. I'm on the Senior Cup Team."

He goes, "I don't care if you're the grand wizard in the Jessop County Clavern of the Ku Klux Klan. What were the causes of the First World War, boy?"

I shrug my shoulders, roysh, and I'm like, "Hitler, I suppose." He goes totally ballistic, roysh. He's like, "WRONG WAR, YOU IMBECILE." Then he tells me to sit down, roysh, and he's like, "That's the problem with you rugby lot. You concern yourself too much with what's between your legs and not enough with what's between your ears. I want a full, detailed proposal of what you plan to do for your special topic on my desk at ten o'clock in the morning. Do I make myself clear?" and I'm just there going, 'You are focking totalled'.

After class, roysh, I head up to Father Feely's study and, like, tell him what happened, roysh, and he goes totally ballistic, and we are talking totally here.

He's like, "Are you telling me that a member of the Senior Cup Team was treated disdainfully by a teacher?" I'm like, "Yeah."

He goes, "WELL, I AM NOT PREPARED TO STAND BY AND ALLOW THIS TO HAPPEN IN MY SCHOOL." And he storms off, roysh, and goes down to, like, the staff room and, according to a couple of the goys who were standing outside, he focks Coffey out of it, gives him a major bollicking, and we are MAJOR here. Feely comes back about ten minutes later, roysh, and he's like, "How far to you want to press this, Ross?"

I'm like, "What do you mean?"

He goes, "I can dismiss him now, or suspend him pending a disciplinary hearing, or I can-"

I go, "No, it's cool. An apology in front of the class will do."

Feely's like, "Oh, you'll get your apology, make no mistake about that. I'm just so very sorry it happened."

I leave his office, roysh, and I'm heading down the corridor and I see this poster, roysh, and it's only, like, then that I realise what Joanna meant when she said she'd see me on Tuesday. It turns out we're doing a production of *My Fair Lady* with, like, the Whores on the Shore, roysh, and they're all coming to the school this afternoon for auditions.

I'm there going, 'Okay, let's rip the TOTAL piss'. None of the goys on the team are going, roysh, they're all going to the gym instead, but I persuade Christian and JP to, like, come with me and Terry's already going because he wants to see Gemma Maynard, this total babe who he snogged two weeks ago in the rugby club, and Oisínn is also going because he is into Diardra Deevy, who's, like, her best friend. The auditions are in the assembly hall, roysh, and me and the rest of the goys go along and we're, like, ten minutes late, and when we walk in, all the girls are, like, turning around and they're all there going, 'Oh MY God, WHO are they?'

Miss Kennedy, who's, like, the drama teacher, roysh, she goes, "I'm glad you could join us, lads, however late. It's good to see so many of you interested in the dramatic arts." We're there going, 'Yeah, roysh. As if.' All the girls, roysh, are breaking their shites laughing as Kennedy tells us all to come up and sit at the top of the room and we all, like, walk up, you know, playing it totally focking Kool and the Gang.

Anyway, roysh, Kennedy calls for volunteers to sing, like, a scale, and then to sing *Amazing Grace* while she accompanies them on the piano. There's probably four hundred people in the hall, roysh, and there's only about thirty who want to be in the play or musical or whatever the fock it is. Only knobs put their names forwards for these kinds of things. The rest of us are just, like, sitting there, sussing out the talent.

Christian's like, "Oh my God, Ross, there's that one you were with. The night I was with Keelin."

I'm like, "Who?"

He goes, "Oh, what's her name? Joanna."

I'm there going, "Which one?"

He's like, "The one up there on the stage, second from left, pink scorf."

I'm like, "Oh yeah. She's GAGGING for me."

Terry looks, roysh, and he's like, "I thought you said she looked like Chloe out of *Home and Away*."

I'm like, "She does a bit."

And Terry's like, "She looks more like Alf from where I'm sitting." And Christian high-fives him, roysh, and then Terry high-fives JP.

Then Christian spots this TOTAL babe, roysh, sitting five rows behind us, totally amazing body, and she looks SO like Posh Spice it's unbelievable. When the auditions are over, roysh, we all break up and all the girls are, like, on one side of the hall and all the goys are on the other and Christian just goes, "I'm going to make the first move if no-one else does," and he heads over to your one, who I have to say was giving him the big-time once-over all afternoon.

I head over with him, roysh, and we introduce ourselves and she says her name is Jill and she introduces us to Evy, who's, like, her best friend and a total stunner. She looks a bit like Gillian Anderson from, like, *The X-Files*.

Jill's there going to Christian, "I saw your picture in *The Irish Times* last week," and Christian's like, "Oh my God, TOTAL shamer".

Yeah, as if. I know for a fact that Christian kissed four girls last Saturday night on, like, the strength of that photograph.

Evy's like, "No, it was a really nice picture. I don't really know much about the rules of the game, but it was supposed to be a totally amazing try as well."

Evy turns around to me and she's like, "You were with Joanna Mulhall, weren't you?"

I'm there going, "Oh MY God, how did you know that?"

She goes, "She told everybody."

There's a bit of a silence and then she's like, "I'm not being a bitch or anything, but nobody could believe it when they heard you were, like, with her."

I'm like, "Why?"

She goes, "Well, she's really sound and everything, but she's-"

Jill interrupts, roysh, makes an L shape with, like, her thumb and her forefinger and then in an American accent goes, "LOSER".

Next thing, who's standing, like, ten yords away, like a little focking puppy dog, only Joanna, roysh, so I, like, head over to her and she goes, "Hi-how-or-ya?" and I'm there, "Hi".

She says we seem to be, like, missing each other a lot lately and asks why I never have my mobile turned on, roysh, but she says that that's okay because she's been SO busy helping to, like, organise the pre-debs, roysh, and oh MY God, our CAO applications are due in soon and she already KNOWS she's not going to get what she wants because she hasn't, like, done a tap all year and she's going to have to do some serious cramming between now and the Leaving.

I'm there going, 'You are a TOTAL retard'.

Then she's like, "Listen, one of the reasons I was ringing was – oh MY God, this is SO embarrassing – but I wanted to ask you whether you'd come to the pre-debs with me."

I'm just there, "No."

And she's like, "I understand. You're probably trying to focus on your grame and –"

I'm like, "No, you don't understand. I was with you once. It was a focking beer goggles job. I've no interest in you. End of story." And she, like, bursts into tears, roysh, and runs out of the place and one of her friends, like, runs out after her.

I come back and Christian, like, high-fives me, and Evy, who's smiling, is like, "What a spa," and Jill goes, "She will SO not want to come into school tomorrow."

Evy is eating a bag of popcorn and Jill says she is SO storving and she dips into it at, like, regular intervals. Christian turns to me and he's like, "Ross, who did I say Jill looked like when we saw her earlier on?"

I'm like, "Posh Spice."

And Jill goes, "Oh MY God, you are about the tenth person to say that to me since I got my hair cut."

We ask the girls whether they fancy going for, like, a few scoops later. Jill says she has no clothes with her and she lives in, like, Greystones, but Evy says they can go back to her house in Blackrock and she can borrow something or hers, and Jill says yeah, as long as it's her new baby blue FCUK top and Evy's like, "As if".

Jill says no, she's only joking, she'd rather go home to get changed anyway, because she wants to wear her new black camisole top by Warehouse, so she phones her old dear on her mobile and asks her to come and collect her. We tell them where we'll meet them and head off. As we're walking away, I can hear Evy saying, "Oh MY God, I don't want to be a bitch or anything, but I can't BELIEVE how much weight Claire O'Loughlin has put on."

* * * *

I HAVE four new messages. Keeva, says she's sorry for flying off the handle in her last message, that I must think she is a TOTAL spa and she understands that I'm probably too focused on my game to get too involved with anyone at the moment. She says that when it's over, perhaps we could go for a drink or to the cinema or something, then she says thanks for the advice on what song she should choose for the graduation, that they're actually going to do *One Moment in Time* by Whitney Houston, which wasn't her idea, it was Jade's, and Jade is such a TOTAL lick orse that Miss Holohan would ACTUALLY take her word over the word of the deputy headgirl, HELLO?

Sorcha rang twice to say that she needs to speak to me urgently and we are talking totally urgently. And Simon, the team captain, rang to say he wants to meet up and have a chat about the semi-final against David's, which is only, like, two weeks away.

I ring him back, roysh, and we arrange to go for, like, a sauna at Riverview, where his old man's a member. I get up, roysh, have a shower, put on clean Calvin Klein boxers and I have a glass of orange juice while I'm, like, trying to decide what to wear. I think about wearing a Harlequins rugby shirt, blue O'Neill's tracksuit bottoms and navy Dubarry Docksiders, but I don't want to have to, like, come home and get changed if Simon suggests heading into town for a few scoops. I end up wearing a navy Armani v-neck jumper over a white shirt by Ralph Lauren, tan coloured deckpants by G-Star, brown Docksiders by Pepe and a navy sailing jacket by Henri Lloyd. It's, like, a good job I did, roysh, because Simon has, like, got all dressed up when I meet him in the lounge. He's wearing a charcoal grey mock turtle neck jumper, grey Diesel jeans and brown Docksiders by Dubarry.

When he sees me, he goes, "Yoh Ross, my man", and, like, high-fives me. We go into the bor, roysh, and we both order a Diet Coke and he asks whether I heard about Terry. I say I haven't, roysh, and he tells me that Terry red-carded Aoife last night, up at the rugby club. He says she's, like, too much of a head-wrecker, that Fionn had already warned him that she was focked up, but he didn't listen. He says all the goys are pretty worried about her.

I'm like, "What the fock was Terry doing in the rugby club on a Friday night. It's, like, SO transition year."

Simon finishes his Diet Coke and he's like, "I know, it's totally full of kids."

We go into the sauna, roysh, and Simon gives me this big chat about our next match, how much important it is, not just for the goys but also for the school and the school's name, and how much is riding on my kicking.

He's like, "If you think about the S as, like, one big machine and all of the players as, like, cogs, you are, like, the most vital cog all. SO much depends on your kicking, Ross."

I'm there going, "Yeah, I know."

He's like, "I just want to make sure you're focused, that parents, teachers, whatever aren't, like, on your case about homework and shit."

I'm like, "No, it's cool."

After the sauna, we play a couple of frames of snooker and Simon asks whether I've heard about Thursday night.

I'm like, "What about it?"

He tells me that he snipped Wendy O'Neill, this TOTAL babe, who's, like, second year commerce UCD. I high-five him and he tells me she phoned him last night and, like, asked whether he'd go to the Comm Ball with her, but he said he'd have to think about it because he didn't really want to get involved in all that heavy relationship stuff while we were still in the cup.

I'm like, "But what a TOTAL babe. She looks like Liv Tyler."

I ask him whether he fancies going for a few scoops, but he says he promised his old dear that he'd collect his sister from the orthodontist at three o'clock, so I tell him I'll probably see him in the boozer tonight.

I'm just getting into my cor, roysh, when my phone rings and like a total spa I answer it. It's, like, Sorcha, roysh, and she's being, like, totally hostile. I'm playing it cool, roysh.

I'm like, "Hey, Sorcha, how's it going?"

She goes, "Why haven't you returned any of my calls?"

I'm like, "Hey, chill out, Sorcha."

She's like, "Why haven't you phoned me?"

I'm like, "Well, in case it's escaped your attention, Sorcha, we're not ACTUALLY going out with each other anymore."

She storts crying, roysh, and she's like, "You are a TOTAL ass-hole."

I'm like, "You don't own me, Sorcha. You might wish you did, but you don't."

And she's there going, "I told you there was something urgent I needed to talk to you about and you couldn't be orsed even ringing me back."

I'm like, "Well, what is it?"

She goes, "I can't tell you over the phone. I want you to call up to the house."

I'm like, "If I get a chance, I will."

She goes, "No, Ross. Not if you get a chance. If you're not up here by seven o'clock tonight, I'll tell you what I have to tell you in Annabel's in front of all the goys. I'll make a total show of you, Ross, I swear to God."

I'm there going, "Okay, I'll call out to you tonight." And she hangs up, roysh.

It's only then that I remember that it's, like, Valentine's Day on Monday and Sorcha probably has a present for me, although I hope if it's aftershave it's Cool Water by Davidoff, and not cK One, which is, like, SO last year at this stage. I stop off in Stillorgan and buy her, like, a cord, and when I get home, roysh, I go to the fridge, and take out this massive box of Leonidas, which the old dear got from one of the neighbours to thank her for her work as chairperson of Foxrock Against Total Skangers. I tear off the message, write some shite on Sorcha's cord about being the one who has always loved her and will always love her and then go upstairs to get changed. I'm, like, gagging for my bit at this stage and, even though she's having, like, a total eppo at the moment, I'm reasonably confident of scoring her. I put on the black ribbed polo neck sweater by Sonnetti, which she really loves, chocolate-coloured Armani jeans, black penny loafers by Hugo Boss and my navy sailing jacket by Henri Lloyd.

I stick the cord and the chocolates inside the my jacket, roysh, and I'm on the way out the door when I notice the old pair coming across the driveway. The old dear is, like, laden down as usual with bags, from Pia Bang, Richard Allen and Fabio's. When she sees me, she's like, "We've been shopping, Ross."

I'm like, "No shit, Sherlock?"

The old man puts his arm around her shoulder and he's like, "The old credit card took a bit of a hammering, didn't it, Darling?" and they both stort laughing. I just totally blank them, roysh, and start walking away and the old dear's like, "Someone called Suzi phoned last night. She sounded like a really nice girl. She wants you to phone her back today. After five because she's got a hockey match in the afternoon."

I'm like, "Yeah, whatever."

Then she's like, "Are you going out somewhere?"

I'm there, "I'm going to Sorcha's gaff."

She goes, "How are you getting there?"

I'm like, "I'm swimming, you spa."

The old man's like, "Ross, don't speak to your mother like that. We're just wondering which car you're planning to take."

I'm like, "The Lexus".

He's there, "Ross, we're been through this before. The roads around Killiney are far too narrow for you to be driving that car. Why don't you take your mother's?"

I'm like, "I am NOT arriving at Sorcha's house in a Micra."

He goes, "What's wrong with the Micra?"

I'm like, "It's a focking spa's cor, that's what's wrong with it."

I just walk away, roysh, and the old man shouts after me, "Well, take the Lexus, Ross, but drive it to the station and get the Dart the rest of the way. Those roads are far too narrow."

I'm there going, 'Yeah, roysh. As if'.

I drive straight out to Sorcha's gaff, roysh, and I notice that her old man's cor isn't porked in the dirveway, although Aoife's Golf GTI is. She's probably, like, giving Sorcha advice on how to play it cool when I arrive. I ring the bell, roysh, and it's Aoife who answer the door. She's wearing a pink and white cheesecloth shirt by Tommy Girl, light blue boot cut jeans by Hobo, black boots by Nine West and a black sleeveless bubble jacket by Tommy Hilfiger. She doesn't look the best, I have to say. She's lost LOADS of weight and she looks a bit pale.

She looks me up and down, roysh, and she's like, "You are an asshole" as she puts another handful of popcorn into her mouth.

I'm like, "Fock off, you total spa" and she gets into her cor and drives off. I go into the house and Sorcha's, like, standing at the door of the kitchen.

I'm like, "Hi, Sorcha."

She's like, "Hi".

She's wearing a white Ralph Lauren airtex with the collar up and O'Neill's tracksuit bottoms and no shoes or socks. I notice that she has make-up on, thinly but carefully applied. The whole thing, the clean white t-shirt, the bare feet, the understated use of foundation, they all say that she wants to look well but doesn't want to look as though she's made the effort. Girls think this is, like, a trade secret or something, but any goy worth his salt knows about it. She's obviously decided to stort off playing hord to get tonight.

I'm like, "Are your parents in?"

She goes, "No."

I'm like, "Have they gone out for the night?"

She's like, "They've gone to the Cayman Islands."

I'm like, "On holidays?"

She's like, "HELLO? Course not on holidays. Dad has to talk to his solicitor."

I'm like, "Oh my God. The tribunal?"

She goes, "What the fock do you care, anyway?"

I'm like, "I do care, Sorcha. I care so much for you. I really miss your friendship."

She goes, "Don't start, Ross."

I go to hand her, like, the cord and the chocolates and I'm like, "I bought these for you. For Valentine's Day."

She just turns away, roysh, and goes into the sitting-room and I follow her and leave the cord and the chocolates on the table. She turns on MTV and I sit on the sofa next to her and she's like, "Get the fock away from me. You make my skin crawl", and she get up and moves over to one of the armchairs.

We sit there for, like, ages saying nothing, roysh, and that song *Never Ever* comes on and I'm there, like, trying to work out which one of the All Saints Robbie Williams is knobbing when Sorcha turns around and she's like, "I heard you were with Evy Stapleton."

I'm like, "Who told you?"

She goes, "Word gets around."

I'm like, "Do you know her?"

She goes, "Her sister's in my class. So, are you going out with her?"

I'm like, "Just seeing her."

She goes, "You know she was with Gavin Ryan in the POD on Saturday night."

I just, like, shrug my shoulders. She doesn't say anything else for, like, ages, roysh, so I go, "Have you a problem me being with her?"

She's like, "No. I just can't believe you've lowered your standards."

I've been there, like, the best port of half an hour at this stage, roysh, and there's not a focking sniff of score, so I'm getting a bit pissed off with the whole scene.

I'm like, "Look, Sorcha, you don't own me. Okay, we were with each other at the Orts Ball, but that was one night. End of story. I'm a free agent, Sorcha. I can be with whoever I want."

She turns around in the chair, roysh, and she stares at me, like, really cold, roysh, and she goes, "I'm pregnant, Ross."

I feel my whole body go cold and it must be ages before I say anything, roysh, because Sorcha has, like, turned back to the television and now she's watching *Porty of Five*, and finally I go, "You're what?"

She's like, "Pregnant, Ross."

I'm like, "How?"

She goes, "I know you're on the senior rugby team, Ross, and you probably haven't got your teeth into the biology syllabus yet, but I'm pretty sure even you know the basics."

I'm there going, "You said you were on the pill."

She's like, "I was on the pill. But even with the pill, there's still a tiny chance."

I'm like, "Oh my God, this is SO unfair."

She goes, "Well, it might be a one in a thousand chance, but it's happened and it's a fact now."

I'm like, "How come you're so calm about it?"

She goes, "I've had a few weeks to come to terms with it."

I'm like, "Have you told your parents?"

She's there, "Not yet."

I'm like, "Oh my God, don't tell them, whatever you do."

She goes, "HELLO? I think it's going to become a bit obvious after a while, isn't it?"

I'm like, "Hang on a minute. You're not thinking of having it, are you?"

She goes, "Yes, I am going to have it, Ross. I'm having it."

I'm like, "What about college?"

She's there, "I'll have to defer for a year."

I'm like, "But wait a minute. Have you even THOUGHT that maybe I don't want to have a baby. I'm only 18."

She's like, "Look, Ross. It's my choice and I've already decided."

I'm like, "Oh, have you?"

She goes, "Yeah."

I'm like, "How can you even be sure that it's actually mine?"

She goes TOTALLY ballistic then, and we are talking totally here. She's like, "BECAUSE I DO NOT SLEEP AROUND. I AM NOT A SLAPPER. I AM NOT EVY FOCKING STAPLETON. THAT'S HOW I KNOW."

I'm there going, "Okay, just calm down. Calm down, Sorcha. We'll deal with whatever we have to deal with together."

She goes, "No, we won't."

I'm like, "What?"

She goes, "Ross, I'm only tell you this because Aoife said you had a right to know. When the baby's born, I don't want anything to do with you. I'm going to bring it up myself, with no help from you."

I'm like, "That's not what you really want, Sorcha, is it?"

She goes, "It is. Now please leave, Ross."

I'm like, "I'm not leaving you alone."

She goes, "GET THE FOCK OUT OF MY HOUSE."

I get up and walk out.

My head is, like, totally wrecked, roysh. I get into the cor and just, like, drive. I don't even know where the fock I'm going. My head is just, like, in bits. The old pair will go totally spare when they find out and we are talking totally here. I'm not even looking at the road at this stage. I hit this narrow right bend at about forty and at the last minute I notice this, like, Peugeot 203 coming in the opposite direction, roysh, and I swerve to avoid it and end up hitting a wall. The goy in the Peugeot doesn't even focking stop. I get out, roysh, and check the damage. The whole front of the cor is totaled and we are talking totally here. The old pair are going to have a total knicker-fit. I'm getting back into the cor, roysh, when this spa pulls up in a Mondeo, winds down his window and goes, "That's some bang you've taken there."

I'm like, "No shit, Sherlock."

He goes, "You'd want to be careful on these roads. They're very narrow, you know. Probably a bit too narrow for a car like that."

* * * *

THEY'RE showing the early ones on Network Two, Evy says. Or is it Sky One? Whatever it is, it will soon be possible to watch *Friends* 24 hours a day, she says. And Christian says it already is, because you can get them all on video, and Evy throws a playful punch at him and calls him a retard. Jill says she's going to the toilet and Evy automatically stands up to go as well.

Christian's like, "There go the piss posse," and it's loud enough for Jill to hear and she turns around and, like, tells him he's SO dead when she gets back, and Christian laughs inwardly, knocks back about a third of his pint in one go and goes, "Why do you suppose women piss in twos?"

I'm, like, pretty sure I know the answer to that one. In this case, Evy and Jill have gone to the toilet to renew the Issey Miyake, to discuss how quiet I am tonight and what that quietness means for me and Evy's relationship status, and maybe even to compare my merits and demerits with those of Gavin Ryan.

I'm like, "Did you hear who Evy was with on Saturday night?"

He goes, "Yeah. That's cool, though, isn't it?"

I'm there, "Yeah. I mean, we're not actually going out together."

Christian goes, "Jill was with Mark Butler."

I'm like, "Who told you?"

He's like, "I was there. I was in the POD on Saturday night."

I'm like, "It didn't bother you, seeing them together?"

He finishes his pint and he's like, "Nah. We're only seeing each other. Use and abuse, that's the name of the game, Ross. Sure, I was with Nicki Corcoran."

I'm like, "Nicki as in Nicki who used to go out with Fionn."

I think Christian senses that he should feel bad about this, roysh, because he won't, like, make eye contact with me. He just, like, stares at his empty glass and goes, "An erect micky and all that... What's the matter with you tonight, anyway. You're totally out of it."

I'm like, "Take one guess."

All of the goys know about Sorcha, though I haven't told the old pair yet, and I doubt if she's told hers because they'd be, like, straight around to gaff if they knew.

I'm like, "I just can't get my head around it. I'm, like, SO not ready for this shit."

I know Christian doesn't want to talk about this because he, like, shakes his head a bit too enthusiastically, says the words "total bummer" two or three times and then, like, asks whether I want another pint. I say no, but the girls arrive back with another round.

I notice for the first time that Evy actually looks well tonight. She's wearing a red v-neck cardigan top by French Connection over a white halter neck by Elle, black hipsters from InWear at Airwave, and blue chunky runners by Skechers. Jill is wearing a baby blue long sleeved top by French Connection with an FC2K logo on the front, indigo blue boot cut jeans by G-Star, black boots by Nine West and a baby blue bubble jacket with grey fleece collar by DKNY. I feel like a TOTAL knacker in a biscuit coloured Calvin Klein sweatshirt, navy O'Neill's tracksuit bottoms, brown Dubarry Docksiders and a bottle green fleece by Timberland, especially seeing as Christian really made the effort. He's wearing a white Polo Sport airtex with the collar up, a light grey jumper by Hugo Boss, dark grey Armani jeans, black penny loafers by Marc O'Polo and a baseball cap with the RL logo on the front.

It's, like, SO obvious that I haven't made the effort and Evy has obviously picked up on it, because she's, like, totally ignoring me now. I stand up and Jill asks where I'm going and I say I'm feeling a bit shabby and I need a bit of air. I leave, go into the lane beside the boozer and ring Sorcha's mobile. There's, like, NO WAY I'd chance my orm ringing her gaff, even though I'm pretty sure she hasn't told her old pair yet. Her phone is still switched to, like, the messaging service.

I leave her one, just saying that I'm, like, thinking about her and, like, wondering whether she's told her parents yet, and I tell her we

SO need to talk because we've got, like, loads to sort out and shit. Then I say I hope she can, like, make it to the game on Wednesday and I tell her I'll, like, score a try for her and one for the baby as well. I don't bother my orse going back to the boozer. I just, like, head off in the direction of the bus stop. It's only when I'm, like, on the 46A that I think about the message I've just left and what a total spa I'll probably sound.

4

I

T would NOT be an exaggeration to say that I'm totally kacking it when Simon stands up to, like, make his speech, roysh, and I realise that having breakfast at the school this morning was a total waste of time, and we are talking totally here. We're all, like, SO nervous we can't keep anything down. Fionn is in trap one and Newer is in trap two, borfing their chicken and pasta back up, and Sooty, who's, like, really storting to freak us out, roysh, he's down on his hands and knees and he's, like, slapping the floor and, like, shouting under the gap at the bottom of the doors: "Cough it up, goys. Cough it up. Nerves are good. Channel that energy. Channel it."

Simon gets up, roysh, and he goes, "Sooty's right, goys. Nerves are good. This is a big game. It's massive. Gerry Thornley is out there today, which I think shows just how high the stakes are. David's are a great side. You have to be to make it to the semi-finals of this competition. There are no soft touches left. But we're so close now, we can almost smell it. So let's see off these assholes today and let's make sure we're at Lansdowne Road on the 17th of March."

After that, roysh, we all let out a big cheer and I, like, high-five Simon and Christian, and Terry and Newer high-five each other, roysh, and Fionn high-fives Oisinn, and Eunan high-fives me and then hugs me, roysh, and he's going, "YOU THE MAN, ROSS. YOU THE MAN" and I can feel, like, a swelling up against my leg and I push him away and I'm like, "GET THE FOCK AWAY FROM ME, YOU TOTAL FAG".

No-one notices, roysh, because Simon's, like, still trying to psyche us up, and he's like, "Okay, I want ten now, goys," and we all count to ten, roysh.

Then he goes, "C-A-S-T-L-E-R-O-C-K" and we're like, "CASTLEROCK". Then he's like, "Pick the spuds", and we all have to do the actions, roysh, and he's like, "Pull the chain".

At the end of this, roysh, all the goys are going total apeshit, kicking the walls and, like, punching the lockers. I'm just sitting there with my towel over my head, focusing on my game.

We run out, roysh, and the crowd are, like, SO up for this game. Even before the stort, they're like, "ATTACK, ATTACK. ATTACK ATTACK ATTACK." Which is, like, what we do, roysh, and there's only, like, five minutes gone when Fionn scores a totally amazing try, which I convert. But ten minutes later, it's, like, a TOTAL mare when he goes and gets himself sent off, roysh. He's coming out of the scrum and he, like, stamps on one of their goy's heads and, like, the goys ear is, like, hanging off. Fionn storts arguing with the ref, roysh, and he's there going, "HELLO? His ear was already hanging off. Christian stamped him earlier." But the referee's just there going, "You're off."

After that, roysh, David's end up, like, pissing all over us. They get three tries in the next quarter of an hour and we are, like, SO lucky to be only 32-28 behind in the last, like, five minutes. They're on the attack again, roysh, looking for another try to, like, seal it, and our supporters are like, "DE-FENCE, DE-FENCE, DE-FENCE", and all of a sudden one of their goys, like, drops the ball and it lands right in front of me. I boot it, roysh, and it travels, like, forty yords down the pitch and I, like, bomb after it, and me and Jonathan Palmer-Hall, who's like the captain of David's, we're both pegging it after the same ball, we're neck and neck, and he's shouting in my ear, going, "YOU HAVEN'T GOT THE PACE, YOU SPA. YOU HAVEN'T GOT THE PACE." But I get to the ball first, roysh, and I give it another boot and it just, like trickles over the line and I dive on top of it, and Jonathan Palmer-Hall lands on top of me and I, like, shove him off and I go, "Who hasn't got pace? Who hasn't got the pace now?"

When the goys finally arrive at the other end of the pitch to congratulate me, I'm just, like, sitting on the ground, holding the ball above my head, and all the goys dive on top of me and eventually the referee comes and tell us that he's adding on any time we waste, but no matter how much he adds on, it won't be enough, because I add the points and we hold out for the last few minutes.

When the final whistle blows, roysh, our fans, like, totally invade the pitch and they, like, pick me up and carry me around on their shoulders and they're like, "ONE ROSS O'CARROLL-KELLY. THERE'S ONLY ONE R0SS O'CARROLL-KELLY…"

It takes me, like, half an hour to get off the pitch. When I finally do, roysh, the old man and the old dear are, like, outside the dressing-room. The old man looks a total spa as usual in his sheepskin coat and that hat of his, and he's got, like, the cigar, and he's going, "Terrific game, Ross. Let's just see what *The Irish Times* has to say about this."

I'm like, "Dad, just give me sixty notes, will you?" He takes out this massive wad, roysh, and he, like, peels off three twenties and hands them to me.

I just, like, take them, roysh, and walk away and the old dear's like, "Ross, your father took the afternoon off work for this", and I turn around and all of a sudden the old man's phone rings.

He answers it and he's there going, "No. I told you this morning that I didn't get your e-mail. But it makes no difference. I need those figures on my desk by close of business today."

I just look at the old dear and I go, "Yeah, I bet he spent the whole match on that focking thing."

I walk off, roysh, and just as I'm going into the dressing-room, I bump into Jonathan Palmer-Hall, who's, like, just been into our dressing-room to congratulate the goys. When I see him, roysh, I hold my hands up in the air in, like, triumph, and he shakes his head and goes, "you got lucky".

And I smile at him, roysh, and I go, "No, I got the ball."

* * * *

Melissa Horgan, this total slapper from Pill Hill who I was with two weeks ago, left a message on my mobile that's kind of, like, struck a raw nerve. It was left on Thursday night, wedged in between two more of those *Short Dick Man* calls that are going to, like, force me to change my phone number. Melissa said that I'm an asshole and I don't care about anyone else or their feelings and that one day I'd meet someone who I really cared about and they'd treat me like shit and then I'd know how it felt. She's crying as she's saying this and I stort crying as well, because I know she's right and it's already happened. I haven't been able to stop thinking about Sorcha for, like, the past two weeks. Okay, roysh, if the truth be told, I probably only really want her because I know she doesn't want anything to do with me, but it's, like, totally wrecking my head at this stage. She won't, like, return my calls or anything. I thought she might ring after the game against David's, especially after what Gerry Thornley wrote, but she probably didn't even read it.

I make my mind up to go out to the Merrion Centre, even though I know it's a bad idea, to see if she's, like, working in her mum's shop. I put on my white shirt by Henri Lloyd, which I know she really likes, beige khakis by Ralph Lauren, brown boots by Panama Jack and a bottle green Timberland fleece. I hang around outside the shop for, like, ten minutes, roysh, obviously not wanting her old dear to see me, just in case she, like, knows the story. It doesn't look like Sorcha's actually working today, because I can see her mum and her cousin Clara, who's like second year International Commerce with French in UCD, but there's no sign of Sorcha and just as I'm about to move away I hear this voice behind me and it's like, "What the fock do you want?"

I turn around and it's, like, Sorcha, roysh, and she's holding, like, three take-away Cappuccinos.

I'm like, "Hi" and she goes, "I asked you what the fock you want?"

I'm like, "Sorcha, we have things to talk about."

She goes, "It's too late for talking, Ross."

I'm like, "I just came out to see how you've been".

She goes, "You don't give a shit how I've been."

I'm trying to get a sly look at her stomach, roysh, to see if she's storted to show yet, but her eye contact is pretty intense and I know I'd only get sussed. Simon was saying he saw her on the Dorsh during the week, and I asked whether she had, like, a lump and Simon was like, "Doesn't it take months before they stort to show?"

And I'm like, "How the fock am I supposed to know? I've never done this before." Anyway, he said he couldn't really tell because she was wearing, like, a white hooded kangaroo sweatshirt by Tommy Girl and it was, like, really baggy on her. She actually looks really well today. She's wearing a cream, ribbed polo neck by Ralph Lauren, black parallel trousers by G-Star and black slingbacks by Thomas Patrick.

I tell her she's looking well and she says, "WHATever", and then I tell her that I was, like, a bit scared to go into the shop and, like, face her old dear, and Sorcha says she wouldn't blame me.

I go, "Have you told her yet?" She shakes her head and she's like, "It's finding the right moment that's the difficulty. She's got so much on her mind, with dad and the tribunal."

I'm like, "Is it serious?"

She's there, "HELLO? Mum could end up losing the shop, you focking retard."

I'm like, "Sorry, I didn't realise… How are you coping with… You know…"

She goes, "I'm not even thinking about it. I've got too much on my plate as well. I've only got, like, eight weeks until my exams. And I'm, like, totally all over the place with this whole Aoife thing."

I'm like, "Yeah, I heard she was in hospital. How is she?"

Sorcha looks me up and down and goes, "What the fock do you care?"

I'm like, "I do care."

She goes, "No, you don't, Ross. You don't care about anyone except you."

She goes, "That's why I don't want you having anything to do with this baby. You're an asshole. A total dickhead. Not exactly the kind of role model I want for my child."

I, like, look into her eyes for the first time today and, I know she means it. I search for something to say, some thing, anything, that might, like, change her mind, but all I can think to say is, "Did you hear we're into the final?"

And she looks at me like something she's just wiped off the sole of her shoe, and she goes, "Grow up, Ross."

And she looks me up and down and says it again. "Just focking grow up."

* * * *

Father Feely says that education can go hang so long as a boy can outjump his peers in a line-out, punch his weight in the scrum or kick a three-pointer from an obtuse angle when the chips are down. He's, like, standing up on the stage, roysh, and he's there going, "Books, education, learning, they have their place in a young man's life, of course. But not in yours, because you are the élite. You don't ask a pure bred stallion to drag a cart uphill into town, and similarly, we here at Castlerock would never, EVER, encumber such fine specimens with the drudgery of schoolwork. The reproductive system of the spirogyra, the fixed rhyming schemes of a Shakespearean sonnet and the principle industries of the Benelux countries; free your mind of such fripperies. Iambic pentameter, chlorophyll, Maginot Line, hypotenuse; such terms have no relevance to you or your lives."

Fionn turns to me, roysh, and goes, "What the fock is iambic pentameter?"

I'm like, "Don't ask me, I haven't been in maths since, like, WAY before Christmas."

Feely jumps down off the stage, roysh, and storts shaking hands with us. He's going, "Your lives begin today. None of you know where you will be in ten years' time, but in ten years' time every one of you will look back and know exactly where you were on this very afternoon. Many of you will go on to play for rugby clubs and form new allegiances. A good number of you will meet a fellow at your new club who will get you a highly paid yet unfulfilling job that requires you to wear a suit, perhaps in a local bank branch or some other such financial institution, where you'll open envelopes for £30,000 a year. Others will discover that an inability to spell the word lager is no hindrance to getting a job as a rep for a major brewing company if they happen to be your club's sponsors. Some of you will even go on to manage one of your father's companies, but the point that I'm trying to make is that no matter where you are and what you do, you will always be 'Rock boys. We don't have any funny handshakes, no bizarre ceremonial rituals here, but we are a brotherhood, a fraternity, and no matter where you find yourself in the world, and regardless of what trouble you're in, you can always call up a past-pupil, say that beautiful four-letter word and be assured that your problems are at an end. Because Rock isn't merely a school. It's an institution, a way of life, and it is underpinned by rugby, a sport which as you know is the very essence of brotherhood. So go, go forth, young men, be proud to wear those famous black and red hoops, and let's bring the cup back where it belongs."

We all just, like, burst into *Castlerock Above All Others*, roysh, and Feely is, like, bawling his eyes out. He walks around, shaking us all by the hand again, roysh, and when he comes to me he, like, holds his hand out, roysh, but I don't shake it, I just hold my hand up in the air and he, like, high-fives me.

It's, like, a totally unreal moment. Everyone in assembly gets up, roysh. We're talking, like, standing ovation here, and they're all like, *"We'll take the Rhineland, and the Sudetenland..."*

And it, like, totally blows our minds. I have to say, staying over in the school last night has, like, SO helped with the morale of the team. We're all getting on really well. Even Simon is, like, totally chilled out. Christian was, like, giving him major slaggings last night, saying that the fact that his old dear would be presenting the cup if we won was an big enough incentive for us. Simon's old dear is, like, a total yummy mummy. Simon took it well.

We arrive at Lansdowne Road about an hour before kick-off and the noise is already, like, totally deafening. All our goys are up in the stand, singing all the Rock songs, and we can hear them, like, really clearly as Sooty gives us a bit of last minute advice. Basically, he tells us things we, like, already know, that Gorman's College haven't been in a final for, like, ten years and will really be up for the game. He tells us we have to kick ass and then he totally loses it and storts, like, kicking the lockers and screaming "kick ass" over and over again.

The butterflies are, like, SO bad as we walk out onto the field and the roar of the crowd gets louder. We head towards the South Terrace end of the ground, where there's, like, loads of black and white jerseys, and I can hear the crowd chanting my name. I've got, like, a lump in my throat at this stage. It's, like, SUCH a relief when the match storts because, you know, the nerves settle a bit and it's, like, kick ass time. The first half turns out to be a bit of a mare. I kick four penalties from six, but we don't look like scoring a try, though neither do Gorman's and we're winning, like, 12-9 at half-time. On the way out for the second half, roysh, the old man calls me over to the sideline and goes, "You're playing terrific, Ross. Just keep geeing the rest of the goys up."

I'm there going, 'And what the fock would you know about it'. He is SUCH a spa and we're talking totally here. I was in my gaff yesterday afternoon, roysh, and he calls me into the sitting-room, roysh, and he's waching some totally focking ancient match on video, roysh.

I'm like, "What the fock is this?"

And he goes, "It's a tape of Ireland's triple-crown win in 1982. What a player that Ollie Campbell was. That's you, Ross. You're the Ollie Campbell of the Castlerock Senior Cup team."

I'm just there going, 'HELLO? RETARD?'

It's, like, ten minutes into the second half, roysh, and we're all like, 'Oh my God, total mare'. We're all, like, maybe a dozen metres from their line, roysh, and Christian passes to Gicker and it's, like, a total hospital pass, and their goys get down the other end and, like, end up scoring a try, which they also convert, and we're, like, 16-12 behind.

Then we win a penalty, roysh, and it's, like, difficult enough, what with the wind in my face, but I just do my usual thing, which is, like, place the ball, run my hand through my hair, blow hord, take five steps backwards and, like, four to the left, run my hand through my hair again and take the kick, and it sails over to put us, like, a point behind.

Then all of a sudden, roysh, their prop, who's been giving me, like, total daggers all the way through the match, he comes up to me and he's like, "I am going to totally cream you next time you get the ball."

And I'm there going, "Sorry, have you got a problem?"

And he goes, "Tell your friends not the pass to you. Next time you touch that ball, you're dead."

It's only then, roysh, that I recognise who he is. He's, like, the same goy who took my baseball cap off and threw it on the dance-floor in Annabel's a couple of months ago. I was, like, SO close to decking him that night, Simon and Christian had to drag me away. Fionn said he was Alyson's brother. She's this girl I was with, roysh, who's, like, first year law in UCD, total babe, looks really like Zoe Ball, but she's, like, total psycho. We're talking total stalking job here. Anyway, roysh, the referee's getting MAJORLY worried at this stage and he has to, like, pull us aport, and as I'm walking away, I turn around and go, "Your sister's shit."

Five minutes later – TOTAL mare again – they get a totally amazing try from a line-out and we're, like, 'Oh my God, there's only ten minutes left. We're going to lose this'. They miss the conversion but it's still, like, 21-15 to them and we SERIOUSLY need a try at this stage, although they're defending really well. But then it's, like, the last minute, roysh, Fionn intercepts a pass, runs the whole length of the field and scores under the posts. We go totally mental, and we are talking totally here. We're all, like, hugging Fionn and high-fiving each other and shit. I just have the kick the points and the game's in the bag because there's, like, no time for them to come back after this.

I pick up the ball and Simon comes over to me and puts his forehead against mine, roysh, and he, like, grabs the back of my neck and he's like, "YOU THE MAN, ROSS. YOU THE MAN." And all the goys are like, "Kick ass, Ross".

I, like place the ball, roysh, run my hand through my hair, blow hord, take five steps backwards and four to the left, run my hand through my hair again and then… Then I'm, like, gone. My mind is, like, totally gone. Running my hand through my hair reminds me of Sorcha and the cute way she takes off her scrunchy and slips it onto her wrist and then shakes her head and, like, pulls her hair back into a low ponytail again, and the way she pulls those four or five strands out and sometimes puts a couple of them behind her ears. I can't stop thinking about her. My head is, like totally wrecked. I can't hear anything. It's all, like, total silence. I must have been standing here for ages, roysh, because everyone's looking at me as though I'm, like, a total weirdo and I can see that Simon is trying to say something to me, which I presume is along the lines of, 'Hurry the fock up', so I just run and kick it and the second I hit the ball, roysh, the sound returns and it's all, like, groans and I watch as the ball sails high and wide of the posts.

The goys from Gorman's go totally mental, roysh, and I can barely hear the final whistle, but when it goes I just, like, fall to the ground and I'm like, lying there face-down with my head in my hands, bawling my eyes out, and all our goys – Fionn, JP, Oisinn, Christian – are coming over and they're going, "It's not your fault, Ross."

And I'm there going, "I focked it up. I focked it up for every-one." And they're all like, "AS IF. We wouldn't even be here today, Ross, if it wasn't for you."

We go up and get our medals, roysh, and as I'm coming down the steps, Alyson's brother makes an L-shape with his finger and thumb and mouths the word "loser" at me, and then for the first time I notice that Alyson's there, and she's, like, hugging her brother and all the other spas from Gorman's. Then we all have to, like, stand there and watch the retards go up and get the Cup and we're, like, totally in bits at this stage. I'm, like, bawling my eyes out again as we leave the pitch, roysh, and I notice the old pair hanging around the players' tunnel, and the old dear shouts my name and storts waving and making a total spa of me.

The old man is on the mobile and he asks the goy on the other end to hold on for a minute and he shouts over to me, "Don't worry, Ross. Even Ollie Campbell had off-days." And then he goes back to his call. I call him a spa at, like, the top of my voice and go into the dressing-room. All the goys are, like, sitting around, just in bits. Feely comes in and says that now that the Cup is over, we'd better, like, knuckle down to our studies, because the mocks stort in two weeks.

I ask Simon for, like, a quiet word, roysh, and we sit in a corner and I tell him I'm really sorry for focking things up for the team. I tell him I had an attack of nerves. He's, like, totally sound about it and says that we lost it over the full 80 minutes and not, like, on the strength of that one mistake at the end. I ask him what he's going to do now. He shrugs his shoulders and goes, "Repeat?"

I'm like, "You can't repeat again. They're going to suss that you're over-age sooner or later."

He, like, shakes his head, roysh, and he's like, "Maybe they will. Maybe they won't," and then he goes, "Hey, Ross, are you coming to my 21st on Friday night?"

* * * *

Emer, who's like first year Science UCD, says she SO has to change her mobile, and Sadbh, Simon's cousin who's, like, first year Com-merce, reminds her that her old man only bought it for her two months ago and Emer goes, "Yeah, but it only stores, like, forty numbers."

Sadbh is just there going, "HELLO? MISS POPULARITY?" And I make a note in my mind to check my messages, though not yet. Not while I'm still in with a chance of scoring Emer, who's a bit like Alicia Silverstone and looks totally amazing tonight in a grey hooded mohair dress by Jasper Conran and black slingbacks by Guess. Christian is, like, hanging out of Sadbh, and Elinor, who he's been seeing for the past three weeks, is giving him filthies from the bor. Sadbh isn't the Mae West, I have to say, but she does look quite well tonight in a white satin shirt by French Connection, a black pencil skirt by Karen Millen and black knee-length boots by Alberta Feretti, although I can't agree with Christian when he says she looks like Kate Winslet.

Anyway, she's looking around the room, roysh, she takes a sip from her vodka and Red Bull, screws up her face and goes, "Why did Simon have to have it the tennis club of all places."

Sadbh shakes her head and goes "Do NOT talk to me about this place. I have SO let my game go since I storted college. I'm just here going, 'HELLO?'"

Emer is like, "It's not that. It's just, like, SO full of kiddy-nippers. Fiona Manning's little sister is here. HELLO? FAKE ID OR WHAT?" Emer tells Sadbh that Fiona Manning got totally hammered and made a total spa of herself in Hilper's the other night and she ended up with Jonathan Flood, who's, like,best friends with Adam Brennan, who she was going out with for two years.

This is, like, SO boring to me and Christian, who throws his eyes up to heaven and then gestures towards the bor and we head off to get, like, another pint. We're standing there, roysh, and Fionn and Oisinn arrive over and there's, like, major tension between me and Fionn. His old dear is challenging mine for the presidency of Fockrock Against Total Skangers or whatever they're called, and my old man went totally ballistic at his old man in front of half the focking world at the K Club last weekend. Fionn just, like, offers me his hand, roysh, and no matter what happens will never destroy our friendship, and I go, "As if. We've been friends since we were, like, four years old, Fionn", and he gives me a hug and it's, like, cool. Christian turns around to Oisinn, roysh, and he goes, "What's the story, why aren't you wearing the old rugby regimentals?"

Oisinn is the only one on the S who isn't wearing, like, shirt, chinos, blazer and tie, although he looks quite smort in a white button-down shirt by Tommy Hilfiger, navy trousers by Henri Lloyd, navy Dubarry docksiders and a bottle green sailing jacket by Henri Lloyd. He's there like, "It just said semi-formal on the invitation." And Christian goes, "But Simon said he wanted all the goys on the S to wear their blazers. You're SUCH a retard."

Christian gets the drinks in, roysh, and Newer comes over to me and says he has a question for me. He's like, "Is it acceptable, do you think, to wear penny loafers with jeans?" I consider this carefully as I'm knocking back the Heino and eventually I go, "Depends on the colour of the loafers."

He's like, "Black."

I go, "Marc O'Polo?"

He's there, "Or Bally. Whatever."

I'm like, "The penny loafer is a formal shoe by design, I suppose, but its versatility is increasingly being recognised, and it has become synonymous with a casual, preppy look. However, I would issue a word of warning here. Goys can not take the same liberties in this area as girls, who can get away with wearing black penny loafers with any colour jeans, even ice blue 501s. For goys, black penny loafers with jeans is an acceptable combination only if the jeans are black, or possibly grey if they're by Armani."

Newer nods knowingly and all the goys stort clapping, roysh, and that's when I notice that Sorcha has arrived, and I'm like, "What the fock is she doing here?"

Christian puts his orm around my shoulder, roysh, and goes, "Chill out, Ross. I know things aren't good between you, but she's still, like, friends with the rest of the goys."

She walks past, roysh, with Eva, her friend who's studying Montessori in Dun Laoghaire, and doesn't even acknowledge me, so I go totally ballistic and go over and I'm like, "Listen Sorcha, WHAT is YOUR problem".

She's like, "I don't have a problem, Ross. How are you?"

That, like, completely throws me, roysh, and I'm like, "Okay."

Eva says she's going to the ladies and focks off and Sorcha goes to me, "I heard about the final. What a mare."

I'm look into her eyes and I'm like, "Yeah. We are talking total bummer here." Oh MY God, she's, like, totally babe-a-licious tonight. She's wearing a white satin dress from Whistles at Brown Thomas and white, leather mules by Marco Moreo, and she smells of Issey Miyake, which means she must have gotten dressed in Eva's house, because she never usually wears it and Eva always does. Gwendalyn, who's, like, Simon's younger sister, waves over at us and while Sorcha's head is turned, I take a subtle look down at her stomach and notice that she hasn't storted, like, showing yet. I wrap my orm around her waist, roysh, and I go, "Sorcha, what made losing the schools final worse was that I didn't have anyone to, like, talk to about it. That's when I really missed your friendship."

She takes my hand and, like, throws it back at me and she's like, "Nice try, Ross. It might have worked a few months ago, but I am SO over you now."

I'm like, "Come on, Sorcha. We could have an amazing summer together."

She's like, "HELLO? I'm going away for the summer."

I'm there, "Where?"

She goes, "To the States, on a J1er."

I'm like, "The States?"

She goes, "You are SUCH a retard, Ross. I told you ages ago that I was going to South Carolina to work in my uncle's country club. Although, I don't know, I might end up going to Ocean City, just to be with the rest of the girls, a better laugh."

I'm there, "Hold on a second, Sorcha, you told me you were going to the States. But I presumed the baby had changed all of that."

She's like, "What baby?"

I'm like, "Our baby."

She goes, "HELLO? You are SUCH a spa. I'm not really pregnant, Ross. I just made that up to fock up your head." Then she walks off, roysh, and I'm just standing there for ages, in total shock.

Then I'm just there going, 'That is IT. I am going to get totally hammered and score someone in front of her'. First of all, I go over to Elinor, roysh, who's wearing a black polo neck dress by Amanda Wakeley and black slingbacks by Nine West, and we're both, like, totally flirting or orses off with each other on the dancefloor, you know, hugging and giving each other little pecks on the cheek, roysh.

We're talking big-time flirting here, roysh, but when I make my move I totally crash and burn and she pushes me away and storts flirting with Eunan, and I'm there going, 'You're borking up the wrong tree there'.

Then all of a sudden, roysh, Kelly Fitzpatrick, who's, like, sixth year Virgins on the Rocks, is ALL OVER me on the dancefloor, and we are talking totally here. She looks a bit like Denise Van Outen and she's wearing a blue, hooded evening dress by Elle Active and blue sandals by Prada. We end up wearing the face off each other on the dancefloor, and I've, like, got my eyes open, wondering where Sorcha is and if she's looking. After about ten minutes, roysh, Kelly says she thinks she's going to be sick and she focks off to the ladies and I go off looking for Sorcha.

When I find her, roysh, she's sitting on a stool up at the cocktail bor and she's, like, kissing Christian, roysh. I go totally ballistic. I go over and I'm like, "You are a SUCH a bitch to pull a stunt like that on me. You wrecked my focking head for, like, months".

And then I turn to Christian and I go, "Some friend you are", and he's like, "Hey Ross, you know my motto, man". Sorcha tugs playfully at Christian's cheek and goes, "What motto is this then?" and I just turn away and go to look for Simon, to wish him a happy birthday before I head off. I walk outside and this girl, who's, like, totally hammered, grabs my orm, roysh, and she says her name is Claire and she's Kelly's best friend, or she was Kelly's best friend, but now she sees Kelly for what she is, which is a total slapper.

I'm like, "Sorry, what the fock has this got to do with me?"

And she goes, "She was only with you because she knew I was mad about you."

She can hordly stand, roysh, and I steady her and sort of prop her up against the wall and tell her to go back inside. As I'm walking away, she's shouting after me, "Kelly Fitzpatrick. She's SUCH a bitch, Ross. Do you know what they call her in school? Kelly Fits Anything."

I go outside and I stort walking. I walk for half an hour, maybe an hour, I just totally lose track of time. It storts raining and I hail down a Jo Maxi and the driver asks me where I want to go, roysh, but I don't know, so I just ask him to drop me at the hospital where Aoife's staying. I look at my watch and it's, like, still only ten o'clock and I wonder whether she's still up. I ask one of nurses what ward she's in and she tells me that visiting time is over and to come back tomorrow, and even though I don't know what the fock I'm doing here, I end up walking around the hospital for, like, twenty minutes until I eventually find her ward.

She doesn't look too bad, certainly not as bad as I expected. Fionn said her parents decided to get help for her after she totally flipped one night. They came home from the theatre to find her going through the family album with, like, a scissors, cutting herself out of all the photographs.

Aoife is lying on the bed, outside the covers. She doesn't acknowledge me when I come in and sit down on hord the chair next to her bed, just carries on, like, staring at the television without looking as though she's actually watching it. Friends is on, although the sound is off. There's a plate of scrambled egg, cold and untouched, on the trolley beside her bed. We both sit there for about ten minutes without saying anything and eventually I'm like, "How long do you think you'll be in here?"

She doesn't answer, roysh. She just goes, "Have you got any cigarettes on you?"

I'm there going, "I don't smoke, Aoife. You know that."

Eventually, I just, like, give up trying to talk to her and just sit there staring at the television with her, and it's only then that I really how hammered I actually am. I can feel myself storting to cry, roysh, and I'm like, "Why are we all so focked up, Aoife?"

She just goes, "Do you think Courtney Cox's hair would suit me?" and I can't take anymore so I just, like, get up and walk out and as I'm on the way out the door, I hear her whisper, "Bring cigarettes next time."

5

• • •

Y ou CANNOT say that Polo Sport smells anything like cK One, Christian tells Oisínn as he pokes at the embers of the camp fire with a long stick.

He goes, "Polo Sport is a clean citrus scent energised with a crisp sea breeze accord and enhanced by masculine woody notes. cK One is a light, simple fragrance, naturally clean, pure and refreshing, with an intimate combination of brightness and sensuality. You are SOME retard."

Oisínn, who's rooting through his backpack for his flask, goes, "Oh my God, TOTAL shamer, do you know what I'm mixing cK One up with? Fahrenheit. The old man wears it. That is REALLY like Polo Sport."

Christian shakes his head and goes, "HELLO? Get with the pro-gramme, Oisínn. Fahrenheit smells nothing like either cK One or Polo Sport. Fahrenheit is a fresh fragrance containing woody and amber accents enlivened by live florals and the surprise counterpoint of balsamic notes. What is the matter with your nose. You're going to end up wearing, like, Brut if you're not careful. Or Blue Stratos. You spa."

Oisínn goes, "Who are you calling a spa?", and he gets up, roysh, and dives on top of him, but Christian, like, fights him off and get his head and storts pushing it into the snow, and Simon, who has-n't said anything up until, he just, like, flips the lid, roysh, and goes, "ENOUGH. Enough already. Can we just stop fighting among our-selves and, like, try to think of a way out of this."

Climbing Carrantouhill was Sooty's idea. He said it would, like, help build team morale. He'd had it planned for, like, ages, roysh. But the weather had been far too good, but yesterday the Met Office was forecasting temperatures of, like, minus ten degrees, heavy snowfall with intermittent blizzards, and Sooty calls us altogether and goes, "We here at Castlerock have a time-honoured tradition of taking inexperienced and ill-equipped students up to the top of Ireland's highest mountain at the height of winter when conditions are at their most treacherous. If we set off this morning, we should get the worst of it by the time we reach the summit tomorrow."

He, like, insisted, roysh, that we didn't bring a map with us. He was there going, "We don't need one. The emergency services will find us and airlift us off the mountain. It's tradition."

No-one knows where the fock Sooty has gone, though Gicker says he thinks he thinks he set off for the summit on his own at first light, muttering something about us being a bunch of pampered, middle class wusses. So it's left to Simon to, like, try to hold the whole group together.

It's, like, freezing cold, though. I'm wearing a charcoal grey ribbed sweater by Dolce & Gabbana, black jeans by Hugo Boss, brown boots by Timberland and a navy and red sailing jacket with blue fleece lining by Henri Lloyd. Simon looks much warmer in a black ribbed polo neck jumper by Matinique, black jeans by Armani, black boots by Panama Jack and a bottle green fleece by Henri Lloyd, while Christian looks even colder than me in a light blue shirt by Tommy Hilfiger, beige Deckpants by G-Star, brown boots by Timberland and a black fleece by Lowe Alpine.

We're sitting there, roysh, and it's storting to get dork, and we're, like, totally kacking it at this stage, and Gicker goes, "It's no good, lads. We have no strength left. We're going to have to, like… eat each other. Like in that movie."

And Simon goes, "No, let's at least wait until the food runs out."

Christian's like, "Simon's right. We should have enough tack to last us four or five days if we ration it sensibly. Can we run a check on what we have left?"

Terry drags the icebox over to us and goes, "I've already done it. We have 125 paninis; 50 with cured bacon and mozzarella, 45 with basil, tomato and cheese, and 30 with chicken and guacamole, all from M&S, naturally. We have 112 Caesar salads, 60 green salads,108 BLTs, 97 croissants, 104 tubes of Pringles, 38 bags of nachos, 82 American-style muffins and 145 powdered cappuccinos, each with a complimentary amaretto biscuit."

Simon goes, "Okay, we have enough food to last us today and tomorrow then" and Christian's like, "If we do have to eat each other, I'm keeping close to Fionn."

Fionn goes, "Why?", and Christian's there, "Because you're a fat bastard".

Fionn gets up, roysh, and he's about to deck him, when all of a sudden, Newer comes legging it over to us and he's, like, really excited, roysh, and he says he's managed to pick up 2FM on his Walkman radio, and we all sit around and wait for the news, to see if anyone's, like, missed us yet.

Anyway, the goy reading the news, roysh, he goes, "The search for the members of the Castlerock College rugby team who went up Carrantouhill in the middle of a blizzard has been abandoned. In a statement this evening, the rescue services said they'd decided there was no point in risking good men to save the lives of a bunch of obnoxious middle class brats who would probably only end going back up the mountain at the next sign of snow."

Gicker is just there, "NOOOOOO", and all the goys are going totally ballistic, convinced that we're going to die. Then Terry checks the provisions, roysh, and discovers that we're almost clean out of, like, Brylcream and designer aftershaves, and we're going to have to stort rationing them.

Fionn has, like, totally lost the will to live. He's just, like, lying there in the snow, groaning, going, "My quiff… is… falling down… Need… gel…"

And Brad is like, "I smell so bad, man. If I don't get some Acqua Di Gio, I'll go FOCKING crazy, man."

Christian, roysh, tries to, like, take our minds off the whole nightmare by getting out his guitar and storting, like, a bit of a singsong, and he plays, like, *On Top Of Old Sophie* and *The Hairs On Her Dickie-Die-Doh*, and then Simon, roysh, gets us singing *Castlerock Above All Others* and then teaches us, like, the little-known second verse of the song that he learned when he was repeating for the first time five years ago.

And it's like:

We are the chosen ones,
Gilded brats one and all,
Inability to spell our own names
Shall not impede our chances of getting a job
In Dad's company,
Or the companies of any of his golfing friends,
Or the company of any orsehole
Who went to a rugby school
And can't accept the fact
That he doesn't anymore,
Because we play rugby,
We are Castlerock,
Ein volk, ein Reich, ein Rock

And we all stort to feel a bit better, roysh, but before we all, like, crash for the night, roysh, Simon double-checks the provisions and discovers that someone's, like, been at the Tommy. He goes totally apeshit, roysh, and we are talking totally here. He's there going, "Who's been at the bottle? What pig has been at the bottle? Don't you know you're playing with our lives? Why didn't you just slit our throats while we slept?"

Oisinn goes, "I saw Christian hanging around the bag earlier". Chrstian goes, "You are SUCH a liar".

And Fionn is like, "Well, you have to admit, Christian, you do smell pretty good".

And Christian is just there, "HELLO? Tommy is an effervescent, woody eau de cologne. If you knew anything about designer aftershaves, you would know that what I'm wearing a fresh tonic musk. It's called cK be, and I've been wearing it since, like, this morning." Simon narrows his eyes, roysh, and goes, "I'm not sure that I believe you", and he's about to deck him, roysh, when we hear this, like, piercing scream, roysh, and we run over to where it's come from and Rory, our prop forward, is just, like, rooted to the spot and he's staring at Brad, who's holding a bottle of Old Spice.

Brad has totally flipped, roysh, and he's telling us to keep back or he'll pour the whole bottle over himself.

Simon is there going, "You don't have to resort to this, Brad. We'll be recused, honestly. It might take time, but you've got to be strong. Don't put that stuff on you. Don't throw your life away."

Brad is like, "Get away from me. I have nothing to live for."

And Simon, like, just makes a dive at him, roysh, and rugby tackles him to the ground and the bottle, like, falls out of Brad's hand and rolls away to safety. Simon goes totally ballistic.

He's like, "Have we all gone totally crazy? Are we going to descend to this now? Become like animals?"

Then all of a sudden, roysh, Eunan comes up and, like, puts his hand on my orse and goes, "I'm really cold. Could me and you, like, snuggle up together tonight, Ross."

I just, like, let out this scream, roysh, and I suddenly wake up, and my bed clothes are, like, SOAKING wet, and we are talking totally here. I've been having, like, the weirdest dreams lately. I'm not really sure if it's, like, the Creatine, which I've storted taking in, like, the last few days. Totally weird dreams, though. I check my alarm clock, roysh, and notice that it's, like, ten o'clock, and I am SO late for school that I decide not to bother my orse going. I have a shower and then get dressed, putting on a navy Ralph Lauren sweat-shirt with the letters USRL on the front, navy O'Neill's tracksuit bottoms and Dubarry Docksiders.

I go downstairs and the old dear is, like, shocked to see me and she goes, "Ross, you have school this morning".

I'm like, "No shit, Sherlock".

And she's like, "You mean you're not going?"

And I'm just there, "Ten out of ten for observation". The old man has left a note on the table to tell me that Cara Louise phoned last night and he's got, like, a question mork in brackets after her name, and his constant efforts to try to, like, get real pally-wally with me just, like, make me want to borf. The message says she's going to try me on my one, which I haven't had turned on for, like, three weeks now, because I was just getting, like, constant *Short Dick Man* calls, and I dread to think how many messages are on it at this stage. I decide not to bother even checking. I'll just tell the old man I need a new mobile.

The old dear asks me what my plans are for the day and I don't answer her, and when she asks me again, I go, "I just told you I'm going to watch MTV. Are you deaf or something?"

* * * *

Grafton Street is, like, so packed it's unbelievable. I, like, SO hate town when it's like this and I shouldn't have bothered my orse coming in to meet Eimear, this girl I was, like, kind of seeing a few weeks ago, we're talking total babe, the image of Calista Flockhart. She's repeating in the Institute. Anyway, roysh, she drags me all the way into town to meet her for lunch, in the Powerscourt Townhouse Centre, and she goes and brings Tara, her best friend, who's doing auctioneering somewhere in town and who's, like, a total mutt, and they end up talking to each other for, like, the whole thing. I hordly get a word in edgeways, except when Tara finds out that I'm repeating in Castlerock and storts name-dropping various goys she claims to be friends with but who she probably just knows to see.

She's just there going, "Do you know Seán Tyner?"

I go, "Yeah".

She's like, "Oh my God, I can't believe you know Seán Tyner. I used to fancy the orse off him. Is he still going out with Rachel Butler?"

I don't even bother my orse answering her. I just, like, get up and walk off and Eimear calls after me and tells me to ring her later on.

My new phone is a Nokia 6150. I have one message, from Beibhín, who's, like, fifth year Whores on the Shore. We are talking, like, total kiddy-nipper here. I was only with her once and now she's, like, TOTALLY stalking me. I met her, like, a couple of weeks ago, on the Dort, roysh. I was in town and I decided to call out to Fionn, who lives in, like, Sydney Parade. Anyway, roysh, she was there with a couple of her friends, Jane and Ciara, and they all had, like, violin cases.

They were just kind of, like, talking and giggling among themselves, roysh, and one of them, Ciara, turns around to me and goes, "Are you Ross O'Carroll-Kelly?"

I'm there like, "Yeah".

She goes, "You used to go out with Melanie Touhy, didn't you?"

I played it, like, totally cool, roysh. I'm there, "The name rings a bell", and she goes, "She's actually my cousin".

And I'm just there, "Small world". Then Jane points at Beibhín, roysh, and she goes, "She is TOTALLY mad about you", and Beibhín goes red, roysh, and tells her Jane that she is SUCH a bitch and a total wagon. I took this as my cue, roysh, to go over and sit next to them and I'm, like, giving it loads, flirting my orse off with Beibhín, roysh, and I end up completely missing my stop.

The next time I looked up, in fact, it was, like Glenageary, and Beibhín announced that this was her station, and I said I was getting off as well, and we ended up being with each other just, like, sitting on the bench on the platform. After about ten minutes, I was, like, thinking I was majorly in here, roysh, you know, Collars Up, Knickers Down, and all that, but she goes, "I have to go. My mum is waiting outside in the cor", and she asked for my number, which I gave her because, I don't know, it was too embarrassing not to.

Anyway, roysh, in this message she says exactly what she said in the last three she left, that I mustn't have got her last message, she presumes there must be something wrong with my mobile and I should ring her later on if I get this message – but not before eight o'clock, because she's got violin – or if I want I could meet her outside Pearse Street Dorsh station afterwards, she'll be finished at, like, seven o'clock, though she'd give me till, like, half-seven and if I didin't show she'd presume I wasn't going to. She's the one who isn't getting the message.

I'm walking down Grafton Street anyway and who do I bump into, roysh, only Sorcha, and it's, like, the first time I've seen her since she came back from the States. She looks totally amazing, even in, like, a pink, hooded sweatshirt from Gap, navy O'Neill's tracksuit bottoms and docksiders by Pepe, as well as Tommy Girl perfume. I actually look pretty well myself, I have to say. I'm wearing a blue and white check shirt by Dockers, blue chinos by Ralph Lauren, brown Dubarry docksiders and a glacier blue lambswool v-neck, which is, like, tied around my waist.

I'm not really sure what kind of a greeting to expect from her, roysh, but she, like, airkisses me and then hugs me and then, like, tells me I look really well. I'm just there, "Did you have a good time in the States?"

She's like, "Oh my God, Ocean City was, like, totally amazing. We worked really hord, roysh, but we went out loads. It was, like, a really hectic social life. Of course, Sorcha comes back without a penny to her name. Oh my God, I turned into SUCH a piss head over there. We nearly got arrested one night, roysh. Me, Aisling and Kate."

I interrupt her and ask whether she wants to, like, go for lunch or something, and she goes, "I'm supposed to be meeting Mum outside Pamela Scott's at two o'clock, so I've got, like, an hour to kill."

We head down to Fitzer's Cafe and get a table and the service is, like, really quick. I order a beef and vegetable stirfry teryaki and a Coke and she has a brie and camembert baguette with spicy wedges and a Diet Coke.

The food arrives, roysh, and Sorcha goes to me, "I heard you're repeating?"

I'm like, "Yeah" and she goes, "Bummer", and I'm there, "I'd no choice really".

I tell her the Leaving was just, like, HELLO??? We are talking total mare here. The only subjects I managed to pass were Ort and Biz Org.

She goes, "I thought you were in college."

I'm like, "I was".

Well, I say college, but it was, like, LBS. Loaded But Stupid, as the goys call it. It was, like, six grand a year, roysh, and at the end you get, like, a degree in morkeshing from the University of Rangoon, which the old man said his company would definitely recognise. I tell her I, like, really enjoyed it at first, especially the social life, but then it turned into a total mare. There was this, like, major push on, roysh, to try to get state recognition for the college as a legitimate third level university, roysh. So the president calls, like, an assembly one morning and tells us that the lecturers wouldn't be giving us our summer exam papers in November as was traditional at the college. He said they were tired of being treated as a joke by the Department of Education and so we'd have to wait until January to get our papers, which would only give us, like, five months to go to the library and learn someone else's essays from a previous year off by hort.

Eimear, who was doing the same course as me at that stage, she went totally ballistic, roysh. She went, "Excuse me, we've paid good money for our degrees. I think it's a total liberty to expect us to sit exams as well."

And Sorcha says that it all sounds SO unfair, but I think she's actually ripping the piss. I tell her it was, like, no joking matter, because two weeks later, roysh, the college went bankrupt. The old man went spare, of course, going on about pouring six grand down the drain, total scab that he is. He plays golf with a goy who was on the board of the college, who reckons he'll still be able to get me my degree, but that could take ages, roysh, so the spa persuaded me to go back and repeat. Sorcha says it must be SUCH a pain in the orse having to go back, but I tell her it's not because all the other goys are repeating as well, and the old man has promised to buy me a cor if I manage to get more points in my Leaving than I kicked in the Schools Cup final last year.

When the food arrives, Sorcha asks the waitress for a portion of coleslaw, and then goes, "Still, it must have been a total bummer when you heard the college had gone bust."

We hordly say anything while we eat, roysh, and I realise that I am TOTALLY over Sorcha. There's no, like, attraction or anything, but I still want to prove to myself that I could have her if I wanted her, which is, like, a big thing to me. So I stort, like, turning on the old chorm, roysh, and I'm there going, "I've really missed you. I mean, okay, I haven't exactly been, like, an angel since you went to the States, but I thought about you a lot while you were away."

She considers this while she takes off her scrunchy and slips it onto her wrist, shakes her head, pulls her hair back into a low pony tail, replaces the scrunchy and pulls four or five strands of hair forward. Then she takes her Marlboro Lights out of her pocket and puts them on the table and goes, "Are you seeing anyone?"

I'm like, "Yeah, kind of".

She goes, "You either are or you aren't, Ross".

I'm like, "I've been seeing this girl Eimear, who was, like, in my class in college".

She goes, "Eimear who?"

I'm like, "You wouldn't know her."

She goes, "What's her second name?"

I'm there, "Eimear O'Neill".

Sorcha goes, "Small, long blond hair? She was a Mountie".

I'm like, "How do you know her?"

She goes, "She was on the Irish debating team when she was in, like, second year. She was SUCH a good debater".

Then she goes, "So you're only, like, seeing her?" I'm like, "Well, I'm going out with her really, but I don't know. It's not, like, serious or anything".

Sorcha looks at my face, as if searching for something, and then she goes, "You're doing the dirt on her, aren't you?"

I don't answer. I'm just like, "I think I've given up looking for, like, the perfect girl".

Sorcha goes, "Well, I've found the perfect goy".

And just at that moment, roysh, the waitress arrives to clear off the table and it's, like, ages before the focks off, but when she finally does, I go, "Who is he?", but I sound, like, far more worried than I wanted to, and she goes, "Brandon".

I'm there, "Who the fock is Brandon?"

She goes, "Brandon Oakes."

I'm like, "Brandon Oakes sounds like a focking nursing home".

She goes, "Well, he's actually a really nice goy who I met in the States".

I'm like, "Hold on a minute, are you telling me you're over here and he's over there, and you're still going out with the loser".

She stubs out her cigarette in the ashtray and goes, "You're the loser, Ross", and she looks at her watch, which is, like, a pink Baby-G, and goes, "My mom is going to go totally ballistic", and she says it's nice to see me and tells me to call her later and then she, like, leaves me sitting there with the bill.

* * * *

Ultra-resistant. Fantasy ribbed. Studded. Lubricated. Luminous. Extra sensitive for her pleasure. Orange. Strawberry. Fruit of the forest. Egg and focking mushroom. Traditional Irish breakfast. There's too many. It's, like, totally wrecking my head. I drop three pound coins in the slot and choose a three-pack of extra-sensitive, gossamer, ribbed ticklers. On the way out the door, roysh, I take a look at myself in the mirror. I'm wearing a light blue shirt by Ralph Lauren, beige chinos also by Ralph Lauren, black penny loafers by Marc O'Polo and an Armani baseball cap with AJ on the front. I look a bit rough though, a bit shabby. I splash some water on my face and, like, turn the nozzle on the hand-drier upwards to dry it off. Then I go back out.

Angel, who's, like, first year law Portobello, roysh, she's telling Ana with one n that she ACTUALLY didn't want another drink, but Ana with one n, who's also doing law in Portobello, tells her not to be such a knob.

Angel goes, "Oh my God, I am SO not going to be able to get up for water aerobics in the morning".

Ana with one n stops pouring her Coors Light and goes, "Oh MY God, Angel, those Heinz Weight Watchers dinners are TOTAL puke".

Angel goes, "Which one did you have?"

Ana with one n is like, "It was, like, salmon mornay with broccoli" and Angel goes, "HELLO? You're SUCH a retard. I told you to get the Mexican chili with spicy wedges one. Or chicken in peppercorn sauce."

Ana with one n goes, "WHATever", and takes her Candy Kisses lipbalm out of her little, miniature backpack, which is silver and from Morgan.

I've been, sort of, like, going out with Ana with one n for the past two months, roysh, even though I'm not really that John B Keane on her. She's, like, really good looking, a little bit like Cameron Diaz, but I'd much prefer Angel, who I was with in Oisinn's house after his 19th, which was, like, a few weeks ago. She just storted, like, coming onto me and I'm just there going, "A man's gotta do what a man's gotta do".

Ana with one n knows nothing about it, of course, and I intend to, like, keep it that way. Loose lips cost shifts, as Christian says. Ana with one n is ACTUALLY better looking, but Angel's just, like, sexier. She looks a LITTLE bit like Martine McCutcheon, roysh, and she's, like, a TOTALLY amazing kisser. we are talking totally here. Tonight, she's wearing a baby blue, short-sleeved top by Morgan, indigo, buckled-back flared jeans by Gap, white, chunky soled runners by Skechers and a baby blue, sleeveless bubble jacket by Prada. Ana with one n is wearing a pink short sleeved t-shirt by Warehouse, beige combats by Hobo, black Buffalo runners and a black, sleeveless bubble jacket by, I think, Tommy Hilfiger. Even Fionn and Christian agree she's in, like, the halpenny place compared to Angel tonight.

Fionn turns around to me, roysh, and goes, "Ross, are you using creatine this year?"

I go, "Yeah, I thought we all were".

He's like, "No, I'm still thinking about it".

Christian goes, "You are SUCH a wuss".

Fionn's there, "Hey man, they don't know the effect that the stuff can have on you".

I go, "It's only, like, two-and-a-half level scoops of powder in your tea four times a day. And that's only to stort off with. Then you go down".

He goes, "Sorry, goys. That's, like, heavy shit. It's a mug's game".

Christian's like, "Yeah, roysh. As if".

Even though you're not supposed to, like, exceed the minimum dose, roysh, I had a total mare against St Benedict's on Wednesday and I decided to, like, stort taking a little bit more. But it's only, like, forty grammes a day. I can handle it, like.

I go up to the bor and get, like a vodka and Red Bull, and when I come back, roysh, Ana with one n is talking Lise with an e, this total babe who's, like, repeating first year International Commerce with French UCD. She's wearing pink shirt by Tommy Hilfiger with the collar up, ice blue 501s and brown penny loafers by Bally. She's also wearing Issey Miyake perfume.

Lise with an e tells Ana with one n that she SO should go to the Comm Ball in UCD because it's going to be SUCH a laugh and that she can get tickets for anyone she wants because she's on the organising committee. Angel, who can't stand Lise with e because she is SUCH a sly bitch, is telling Christian that she hasn't done a tap all year and is SO going to fail her exams if she doesn't get her finger out of her orse. Christian is definitely going to end up being with her, which makes me, like, kind of jealous, roysh, and I have to get away, so I tell Fionn that I'm heading out onto the dancefloor and he follows me.

The music is amazing, roysh, and it's, like, *Praise You* by Fat Boy Slim, and we're down there giving it LOADS, and I'm flirting my orse off with Rebecca O'Neill, who's, like, first year social science UCD. Looks a little bit like Liz Hurley. I'm there, like, hugging her on the dancefloor and shit, and she's, like, totally gagging for me.

She's wearing a white Calvin Klein top with a black cK insignia on the front, black boot cut jeans by G-Star and black boots by Marco Moreo.

After a while, roysh, she goes, "Where's Simon tonight?" and I'm like, "He's staying in. He says he's staying off the gargle until after the Schools Cup final".

She goes, "He's taking it bit seriously, isn't he?"

I'm like, "Well, he has to. He says he's not repeating again after this year. He can't. He's going to be sussed".

She's like, "So he's not drinking at all".

I nod my head and go, "Total knob, huh".

She goes, "Totally".

Just then, roysh, I look across the dancefloor and I notice this girl I've never seen before and she's, like, staring at me. She's a total babe as well. Looks a little bit like Elle McPherson. She's wearing white shirt by Yves Saint Laurent, dark grey trousers by Karen Millen and black sandles by Nine West. I walk over to her, roysh, and I go, "You're a really good dancer" and she turns around, roysh, and she wriggles her little finger at me, which presumably means she's heard that I have, like, a small penis, which I don't.

* * * *

I wouldn't have bothered, like, sitting the test, roysh. except the old man said he'd get me, like, a red Peugeot 205 GTI (we're talking total babe magnet) for my 19th if I got my full licence. Oisínn told me to do it in some bogger county where it's supposed to be, like, easier to pass, roysh, so I applied to do it in Wicklow. There was no way I was waiting a focking year for it to come up, roysh, so the old man wrote me a letter, saying I, like, worked for one of his companies and needed the car for my job, bullshit, bullshit, bullshit.

Anyway, roysh, I'm sitting in the testing centre and I'm, like, waiting for my name to be called, roysh, looking reasonably well in a white Ralph Lauren rugby shirt with black sleeves, black jeans by Firetrap and brown docksiders by Dubarry.

Then, all of a sudden, roysh, this, like, old fart comes out and goes, "Ross O'Carroll-Kelly", and I follow him into this room, where he asks me to show him, like, my provisional, and then he storts asking me these TOTALLY stupid questions.

He's there, "How do you know when you are approaching a pedestrian crossing at night?"

I'm like, "You just, like, keep your eyes open for, like, people and shit".

He goes, "No, I'm asking you how would you know you are approaching one when it's dark?"

What a TOTAL retard. I'm there, "Sorry, I've already answered your focking question. Anyway, we're in the middle of Bogland. How many pedestrian crossings do you see in an average day down here?"

He just, like, stares me out of it, roysh, and then tells me to follow him outside and we get into my cor – well, dad's cor, the Beamer – and he tells me to drive the way I normally would, roysh, which means he DEFINITELY has it in for me and wants me to fail. Before I put the key in the ignition, I ask him one question, roysh, one simple question, and he goes totally ballistic.

I'm like, "Should I take my baseball cap off?" and he goes, "WILL YOU PLEASE JUST START THE CAR". I am SO going to report this focker if I fail.

We're driving for, like, ten minutes, roysh, and I'm doing fairly alright until he asks me to do a turnaround on this, like, country lane. I'm there going, "I can't. It's too narrow".

He's like, "No it isn't. Please proceed with the manoeuvre".

I totally lose the rag with him then, roysh. I'm like, "HELLO? Are you deaf or something? I said it's too focking narrow".

He goes, "What would you do if you were in a situation where you had to turn around on this road?"

I'm like, "I'd do what any focking normal person would do. I'd find, like, a driveway or something to turn into". But he just can't leave it, roysh, and he's there going, "But what if there is no driveway? What if there were roadworks here, the road ahead was closed, what would you do then?"

He is, like, totally wrecking my head at this stage, roysh, and I just go, "HELLO? How often do you think I come down here? I'm only doing the test here because it's supposed to be easier to pass. Oisinn is SO focking dead next time I see him."

Anyway, I try to put all that behind me, roysh, and I actually drive really well for the next, like, ten minutes. We're on the way back to the test centre and, like, my mobile rings and I answer it, roysh, and it's, like, JP. I'm there, "Yoh, JP. Not a good time, my man".

He's like, "Oh my God, are you still going your test?" I'm like, "Yeah".

He goes, "How are you getting on".

I'm there, "I'm reasonably confident".

He's like, "I won't keep you long, but you will NEVER guess who Gicker was with in the Sugar Club last night".

I'm there, "Who?"

He goes, "Esmé O'Halloran?"

I'm like, "Who the fock is Esmé O'Halloran?"

He's there, "HELLO? Get with the programme, Ross. Orpha O'Halloran's sister".

I'm like, "Second year commerce UCD, plays hockey for Pembroke?"

He goes, "That's her. But that's not the best bit. You will NEVER guess who Christian kissed?"

All of a sudden, roysh, I stort to lose the signal – surprise, surprise, we're out in the middle of focking bogland – and I'm there going, "JP, you're breaking up... JP, can you hear me?"

I snap the phone shut and turn to the tester and I'm like, "Fock, I lost him". And he goes totally ballistic again, roysh. He's there, "Will you please just watch the road. Do you know how close we came to hitting that blue Micra back there?"

I'm like, "No focking way, Jose. I had plenty of room to pass him. If you fail me for that, that is SO unfair."

We get back to the test centre and he comes straight out with it, roysh. He's like, "It's bad news, I'm afraid. You haven't been successful on this occasion".

I'm like, "Was it that calf we hit? Because if it was, roysh, I have to say I don't think he was, like, THAT badly injured."

But he just, like, blanks me, roysh, and storts filling in this sheet of paper with, like, 20 or 30 things I'm supposed to have done wrong, and he hands it to me. I just turn around to him, roysh, and I go, "You are SUCH a focking retard", and I walk out.

On the way home, I hit a red light at Cornelscourt and decide to check my messages. Some girl called Jennie with an ie rang and said that I gave her my number in the rugby club on Sunday night and she hoped I remembered because I was, like, SO drunk and she hoped I didn't mind her ringing but she just wanted to wish me luck in my driving test and wondered what I was doing, you know, later in the week.

The second message is from Angel, who said she SO shouldn't be ringing me because Ana with one n would go, like, TOTALLY ballistic if she found out, but she just wanted to tell me that Christian was, like, a MAJOR mistake, and she hoped that we could...

Then she says I should call her because we SO need to talk. There's also two text messages from Ana with one n. The first is like, "GOOD LUCK IN YOUR DRIVING TEST, CHICKEN", and the second's like, "I LUV U".

I go into my gaff, roysh, and the old dear asks how the test went. I, like, totally blank her.

She asks me again, roysh, and I go, "Are you deaf or something. I said I failed".

She's like, "Oh well, Ross. Most people fail their first time".

I just look at her, then shake my head and go, "Spare me, will you". I go into the kitchen and make myself a cup of tea and cheese sandwich and, like, take them upstairs to my room. I take out my creatine, roysh, and stir about 30 grammes of it into my tea, and then tip about another 20 or 30 grammes onto my sandwich. Then I lie on my bed for, like, an hour, staring at the ceiling and thinking about returning Angel's call.

6

• • •

ULTAN Mac An tSionnaigh is giving me filthies, roysh, and I'm about to go over and, like, deck the focking retard when Simon comes over to me and, like, asks how I'm feeling. I'm like, "I am SO up for this game", and he goes, "You the man, Ross. You the man". The goy is still staring at me, so I just, like, give him the finger, roysh, but he doesn't respond. Ultan Mac An tSionnaigh is a total spa who took my place on the Leinster Schools team last year.

He came up to me before the trials, roysh, and he goes, "You know we're both going for, like the same place?"

I went, "Yeah, good luck".

And he pushes me and goes, "You are SO dead, asshole". Anyway, roysh, I had, like, a total mare at the trials, but I have to say I'm, like, twice the player I was since I storted taking the old Creatine.

We run out onto the pitch, roysh, and head straight down to our end of the ground, and our supporters are, like, giving it LOADS. They're totally drowning out the Queens Hos goys and we are talking TOTALLY here. They stort singing 'Castlerock Above All Others' and me, Christian, Fionn, Alex and JP stort conducting the crowd and it's, like, a totally amazing buzz.

I'm, like, really relaxed, but still up for the game, if you know what I mean. They get a penalty after, like, three minutes, roysh, and Ultan's getting ready to take it and I, like, walk up to him and go, "There's a bit of a wind blowing. Keep it left." Their prop forward, Gavin Healy, this total spa who's going out with Kelly Brannigan, one of the twins, he grabs me by the scruff of the neck, roysh, and pushes me away. Then Simon legs it over and storts, like, pushing him, and this other goy off their team hops in as well, roysh, and Christian's about to deck him when the ref breaks it up and tells us all to, like, cool it.

The kick is, like, SO easy, roysh, but by the time Ultan goes to take it, his head is totally wrecked and he hits it wide.

About two minutes later, roysh, we get a penalty, and it's from, like, a fairly difficult position. I look over at Ultan and I stort, like, pointing to my eyes, roysh, telling him to watch how it's done. I run my hand through my hair, blow hord, take five steps backwards, four to the right, run my hand through my hair again and put the ball over the bor. I run over to Ultan and go right up into his face and I'm like, "DO YOU SEE HOW IT'S DONE? JUST WATCH THE MASTER, ULTAN. JUST WATCH THE MASTER".

Within the next, like, ten minutes, I kick two more penalties, roysh, one which is, like, SO easy, and another which I don't expect to get, but when I do I know there's, like, no way we're going to lose this match.

When Ultan finally puts his first penalty over, all our supporters are going, 'HAPPY BIRTHDAY TO YOU', and I stort applauding them, and they're there going, 'ONE ROSS O'CARROLL-KELLY, THERE'S ONLY ONE ROSS O'CARROLL-KELLY...'

About a minute before half-time, roysh, JP feeds it to me and I play an amazing pass to Christian, who gets over for the try. Needless to say, I add the points and we're, like whipping their assses 16-3 at half-time.

We go back to the dressing-room, roysh, and Sooty has totally lost it. He's just there going, 'CASTLEROCK. CASTLEROCK. CASTLEROCK', over and over again. I go to my bag, roysh, get out my Creatine and go into trap one. I sit on the bowl and tip about 30 grammes into my hand and stort eating it. It's actually quite difficult, though, because it's too drug and my tongue gets stuck to, like, the roof of my mouth, and then I, like breathe some of it in, and I stort coughing my guts up, and I have to go out and take a drink from the tap. All the goys are asking am I okay and I tell them I'm sound, and then Sooty gives us a bit of a talk, and he storts going "KILL, KILL, KILL", as we go out for the second half.

Ultan's head is totally focked. They get a try about ten minutes into the second half, roysh, and he misses the conversion. Christian gets a second try and, like, Simon gets one as well, and then we just, like, take it easy after that and end up winning, like, 36-17. When the final whistle blows, roysh, I feel totally wired, and we are talking totally here.

I stand just in front of the press box and I look up, roysh, and catch Tony Ward's eye, and then I, like, hold my arms aloft and I go, "YOU SAW IT, TONY. YOU SAW IT, NOW YOU WRITE IT", and all the goys are there going, "You the man, Ross. You the man."

I have a shower and get changed. I put on a white button-down shirt by Ralph Lauren, grey jeans by Hugo Boss, brown docksiders by Dubarry and a black ribbed crew neck sweater, which I tie around my waist.

I come out of the dressing-room, roysh, and there's loads of girls hanging around outside in, like, different groups. I head over to Christian, who's talking to these three total babes from Our Lady of Perpetual Pre-Menstrual Tension in Foxrock. Christian introduces me to them, roysh, and it's, like, Elinor, Jessica and Karyn with a y, who Christian was with at Melissa Corcoran's 18th two weeks ago. She's really good looking, as is Jessica, but Elinor is a TOTAL babe. And I mean total. She's SO like Claire Daines it's unbelievable, roysh, and she is ALL OVER me.

She's there going, "Congrats. You'd a super game."

I'm like, "Thanks", and she goes, "I met you before".

I'm like, "When?", and she goes, "Wesley", and I'm like, "Oh, yeah".

She goes, "Oh MY God, I am SO embarrassed. I cannot BELIEVE you remember that".

I haven't got a focking clue what she's going on about, but we're getting on really well, roysh, and she's, like, really touchy-feely, and I am SO gagging for her you wouldn't believe, when all of a sudden, roysh, who shows up only Ana with one n. I'm just there, 'Oh MY God'.

She comes over, roysh, and I'm like, "What are you doing here?" She's there, "Oh, that is SUCH a nice way to greet me, Ross". I'm like, "You know what I mean. I thought you were going to the National Concert Hall with your parents". She goes, "HELLO? That doesn't stort until eight o'clock, Ross".

I'm like, "Did you see the game?"

She goes, "Yeah, you were amazing."

I nod my head and I go, "Thanks", and then I'm like, "It's nearly six o'clock, you know. You're cutting it MAJORLY fine if you're going to make it to this thing".

She looks at Elinor, roysh, and back at me, and then goes, "Actually, Ross, I know I said I had to go to this thing with my parents, but it's, like, a big day for you and I'm sure they'd understand if I cancelled".

I'm like, "No, it's fine."

She goes, "No seriously, Ross, if you really want me to go out with you, I don't mind giving the National Concert Hall a miss."

I'm there, "No, go out with your parents, Ana. I know how much you've been looking forward to it."

Elinor butts in then, roysh, and goes, "What are you going to see?"

Ana with one n goes, "It's, like, the Lyric Opera production of *Nabucco*" and Elinor goes, "Oh my God, that sounds SO exciting", totally ripping the piss out of her, and Ana with one n squints her eyes and, like, gives her a filthy.

Then Ana with one n goes, "Look, Ross, it's up to you. Do you want me to go out with you tonight or what?"

I'm just there, "No".

And she goes, "Okay, FINE", and as she turns to walk away she stops and looks Elinor up and down, then shakes her head and tuts to herself.

Elinor goes, "Oh my God, that girl has got SUCH an attitude problem."

Me and the goys head into the boozer, roysh, while the girls go across to Eddie Rockets and, like, get changed out of their uniforms in the toilets. I'm on my, like, fourth pint by the time they arrive. Elinor is wearing a pink short-sleeved top by Kookai, cobalt blue bootcut jeans by Diesel and brown docksiders by Dubarry. Jessica is wearing a white short-sleeved top by French Connection, a pink mohair shrug by InWear at Airwave, black boot cut trousers by Prada and black boots by Nine West, while Karyn with a y is wearing a tight white and blue frat top by Tommy, rinsed blue stretched boot cut jeans by Gap and blue chunky soled runners by Sketchers.

Anyway, roysh, we all end up going on the TOTAL rip. By half-ten, roysh, I am TOTALLY hammered, and I get out the old extra-sensitive, gossamer, ribbed ticklers and, like, Fionn, roysh, he gets one and he blows it up and puts it on his head. It is, like, SO funny. Then Christian does the same, roysh, and I get the other one and fill it up with, like, Heino, tie it up and fock it at Oisínn, who's, like, up at the bor. OH MY GOD, it explodes everywhere, roysh, and we end up getting focked out. Christian and Fionn are, like, arguing with the bouncers, roysh, telling them it wasn't us, but I'm, like, laughing too much to say anything. Elinor tells one of the bouncers he has an atti-tude problem.

We all hang around outside for a few minutes, trying to make up our minds whether we should, like, maybe head into town or some-thing. Elinor tells me her parents are in Beauvoir-sur-Mer and asks whether I want to go back to her gaff, and I go, "Does the Pope shit in the woods?"

Then I remember, roysh, that I've no condoms, so I sneak back into the boozer through the side door, go into the jacks and get anoth-er packet out of the machine.

It's only, like, me, Elinor and Jessica going back, roysh. Karyn and Christian say they're going into town with the rest of the goys. Elinor lives in Glenageary and her gaff is totally amazing. We are talking totally here. We go in, roysh, and she makes us all coffee and there's this whole focking girly chit-chat thing going on between Eli-nor and Jessica, who are apparently planning to travel around Spain and Portugal after the Leaving with 28 other girls from their class. Jessica asks me whether I know anyone who goes to Foxrock and I tell her I know Claire Croft and she goes, "Oh my God, I can't BELIEVE you know Claire Croft. She's in my furniture restoration class. She's one of my best friends."

Then she goes, "Who else?"

I tell her I know Susan Travis and she goes, "Oh MY God, you know Susan Travis? She's our head girl this year. I can't BELIEVE you know Susan Travis". Then she asks me about goys in my year who she knows. I go through the motions, but pretty soon I'm, like, SO pissed with this that I'm thinking of heading off home. But I feel like kissing her then, roysh, when she turns down the offer of yet another cup of coffee and says she's off the bed. As she's going out of the kitchen, she's like, "Enjoy yourselves, goys".

As soon as she's gone, roysh, me and Elinor are ALL OVER each other. We're, like, totally wearing the face off each other. She leads me by the hand into the sitting-room, roysh, and we lie down on this, like, white, furry rug her old dear brought back from Canada last year. She opens my shirt, unties my jumper from around my waist and then unbuttons my jeans, while I take off her top.

She goes, "Do you have condoms?" and I'm like, "Yeah", and I go to the pocket of my jeans and take out the little packet.

It takes me ages to find the opening in the cellophane, roysh, but I finally get the box open, and I am totally gagging for it at this stage, and I empty the contents of the packet onto the rug, and it's, like, a comb, a shoe wipe, a tiny toothbrush and a miniature tube of toothpaste.

I'm like, "Oh my God, I must have gone to the wrong machine. I am SO embarrassed". She just laughs, roysh, and goes, "Come on, let's just go to bed", and we go upstairs and fall asleep together.

It's about, like, half-eight when I wake up the next morning, roysh. I want to get the fock out of there without waking Elinor up, roysh, which is difficult because she's lying on my orm. I am SUCH a master at this particular move, though, that the goys call me The Coyote. It was, like, Christian who came up with the nickname. He watched this programme on the National Geographic channel, roysh, and it was all about, like, wild dogs and shit, and it said that if a coyote gets his paw caught in a trap, roysh, he chews off his own leg to stop himself being captured. Well that's me. Christian goes, "You'd chew off your own orm rather than face having to talk to her in the morning". And he's roysh. I get dressed as quickly as I can, sneak downstairs and shut the front door quietly behind me.

I get home, roysh, and the old man's in the kitchen, pouring himself a bowl of muesli, and he goes, "Have you seen it yet?" I'm like, "See what?"

And he hands me *The Irish Times*, roysh, and there's a photograph of me, like, celebrating at the end, and the caption underneath says, "Ross O'Carroll-Kenny salutes supporters after helping Castlerock to victory against Queen's Hos yesterday".

The old man goes, "That is it. I am ringing that newspaper right now." He gets onto the sports desk and storts giving out yords, and the goy on the other end, like, promises to print a correction in Monday's paper.

The old man goes, "I want it on the front page of the sports section. And you can bloody well print the photograph again as well. Otherwise, you'll be hearing from my solicitor." When he gets off the phone, he tells me not to worry, because Tony Ward, a REAL journalist, he says, managed to get my name roysh.

He's like, "Wait until you read what he's written about your performance". As he tries to find the page, he stops and goes, "Oh, by the way. Some girl called Anna phoned for you this morning. It was only about nine o'clock. I said to her, 'You're phoning very early, aren't you?' Very nice girl, though. Very friendly. I went upstairs to get you and your bed hadn't been slept in, so I told her you'd phone her back later."

I'm just there, "Fine".

* * * *

WE should open up a pool, Christian says, or a book or whatever the fock you want to call it, but everyone on the team puts in fifty notes, roysh, and whoever ends up scoring her at the debs wins the lot. Oisínn says that that's presuming she ends up being with only one of us and Christian goes, "It's, like, the first one to kiss her gets the money". And we all agree.

Saturday morning training was a total bummer. We were, like, SO knackered afterwards and Simon suggested we all head out to the driving range just to, like, do something together as a team, keep morale up and shit. It really worked, because after a couple of hours we're all having, like, SUCH a laugh, and when we head on Johnnie Foxes for a few scoops, it's obvious that it's going to, like, turn into a bit of session.

We head into town, roysh, Cafe en Seine, and we are KNOCKING back the pints, and that's when Christian storts going on about Miss Lafayette, our French teacher, who's, like, a focking TOTAL babe. And we are talking TOTAL here. She is SO like Uma Thurman it's unbelievable, small, exactly the same hair, but dorker skin. She is SO gorgeous, but when she gets hammered, roysh, she turns into a total slapper. She's, like, got off with one the sixth years at the last three debs, roysh, and last year, she was with Darragh, one of our backs, in Buck Whalleys. All the goys were giving her LOADS, going, "You are SUCH a slapper".

Christian HAS to stort as favourite this year, roysh. She has, like, a bit of a soft spot for him because his mother is French, but Fionn and Oisínn reckon she's also gagging for JP because she always talks to him at the end of class, asks him what he's doing for the weekend and shit. But I am SO going to try to get in there myself.

Anyway, roysh, we're sitting there and JP's mobile rings and he answers it and throws his eyes up to heaven. We can, like, kind of hear a girl's voice on the other end, roysh, but JP is having none of it. He's just, like, giving one-word answers and shit, it's like, "Yeah... No... Yeah... Yeah... No..." and eventually he hangs up.

I'm like, "Who the fock was that?"

And he goes, "Sally Parker-Holmes".

I'm like, "Carragh's sister? How do you know her?"

He goes, "I was with her a couple times up in Club Knackery-doo. She's on the organising committee for the Debs."

Christian's like, "Is she a Mountie?"

JP's like, "Yeah. Anyway, roysh, she keeps ringing me for advice, you know, do I think they should stort off with a drinks reception at the school, do I think Powerscourt House would be good for the actual debs itself, what nightclub on Leeson Street do I think they should go to."

Oisínn's like, "So why is she asking you all of this?"

And JP goes, "Because she wants me to go with her, roysh, but she doesn't want to ask me. It would be, like, too embarrassing if I said no. She keeps dropping these, like, major hints, asking me who I think she should bring, what about this goy, what about that goy, then she says if all else fails she'll probably end up bringing someone from Clongowes".

We all shake our heads and me, Fionn and Christian go, "Sad bitch", all at the same time.

We're all sitting there till, like, seven o'clock, except Simon, of course, the total knob who headed home at five and said he had to be up early for the gym tomorrow.

All of a sudden, roysh, I hear this voice going, "So this is where you're hiding out", and I look up, roysh, and it's, like, Sorcha.

She looks quite well, I have to say, even though she's only wearing, like, a white Lacoste airtex with the collar up under a pink fleece jumper by Ralph Lauren, white tracksuit bottoms which I think are O'Neill's and brown docksiders by Pepe. She's with her friend Melanie, who's first year engineering UCD, and who's wearing a light grey sweatshirt with a DKNY Athletic logo on the front over a pink Ralph Lauren airtex with the collar up, indigo blue jeans by Diesel and black Buffalo runners.

Melanie storts talking to Oisínn, who she was with, I think in the POD, a couple of weeks ago, while Sorcha comes over to me, roysh, and sits down next to me. We're chatting away, getting on REALLY well, totally flirting our orses off with each other, roysh, which is when I notice she's, like, totally hammered. She's there going on about how her mum is thinking of opening another shop in the Powerscourt Townhouse Centre, and I'm there, you know, pretending I'm really interested. She says she read about my performance against, like, Queen's Hos in the *Irish Independent*, roysh, and goes, "I was really proud of you... God, I sound like SUCH a knob saying that." I'm like, "No, you don't, Sorcha. I liked you saying it". Next thing, we're, like, with each other, roysh, and I can hear Melanie in the background going to the goys, "I knew we shouldn't have come over. I SO knew she was going to end up with him". I can hear Oisínn asking what's wrong with that and Melanie goes, "Because he is SUCH a bastard to women."

Sorcha has, like, NO complaints, though, but eventually it's, like, ten o'clock, and she says she'd better go and get a taxi home, roysh, and I tell the goys that I'm going to walk Sorcha up to the Stephen's Green rank, but the Melanie says she's coming as well because she's saying in Sorcha's gaff, and Oisinn says he might as well walk up too, and in the end we all leave together. Me and Sorcha are kind of, like, lagging behind everyone else, roysh, and I've got my orm around her and she storts all this, like, crying and shit.

She's there going, "Oh my God, I'm supposed to be going out with Brandon. I am SUCH a bitch".

I'm there, "Well, don't tell him".

She goes, "No, that's SO unfair. It's only fair that he knows about us".

I stop walking, roysh, take her arm from around my waist and go, "What's this *'us'* thing?"

She's like, "Me and you".

I'm like, "There is no 'me and you', Sorcha". She looks confused.

She goes, "You just told me you loved me ten minutes ago".

I'm there, "Did I?"

She storts getting all focking hysterical then, roysh, and she's like, "Yes, you did. You did tell me. You are SUCH a bastard, Ross. Why were you with me if you don't have any feelings for me."

I just, like shrug my shoulders, roysh, and go, "Just to prove to myself that I could have you". Then I shout up to Christian and JP and tell them to meet me in Burger King.

I order a bacon double cheeseburger, chips, onion rings, a portion of chicken pick-em-ups and a Coke and sit down, roysh, and after about ten minutes the rest of the goys arrive.

Christian goes, "What's the scan, man?"

Sorcha's going totally ballistic. "Did you two have a fight?"

I'm like, "No, there was no fight. I just told her I didn't want to get serious". Christian shakes his head and goes, "Bummer... Anyway, I'd better go up and get some tack. I am SO storving", and he joins the rest of the goys in the queue.

As if the night couldn't get any worse, roysh, who arrives into Burger King, only Ana with one n and Angel. They're both, like, totally dressed to kill. Ana with one n is wearing a white halter neck top by Elle, blue hipsters by, I think, Sisley, black boots by Pepe and a red bubble jacket by Tommy Hilfiger. Angel is wearing a lilac short-sleeved top by Kookai, denim pedal pushers by Calvin Klein, black sandals by Nine West and a white sleeveless bubble jacket by Ralph Lauren. They're obvious out on the score tonight, roysh, though they do actually look pleased to see me, certainly more pleased to see me than I am to see them. Fionn, who's totally hammered at this stage, storts shouting, "HOW MUCH? HOW MUCH?" at them, and Ana with on n gives a real bitchy smile and the middle finger.

She sits down next to me, roysh, and asks me in why I haven't, like, returned any of her calls. She says this in a really jokey voice, but I can tell she's, like, really pissed off about it.

I tell her I've been busy and she goes, "Too busy even to send a text message?" Angel, who's sitting next to JP and flirting her orse off, goes, "Yeah, Ross. That is SUCH a rude thing to do, not to return calls", and I can't even look at her when she says that. Ana with one n doesn't, like, pick up on it. She's too busy looking over her shoulder at the queue up at the counter.

She goes, "I am SO storving", and Angel goes, "Oisínn, would you be a complete dorling and go up and get me fries and a Diet Coke".

Oisínn, like a total spa, says he will, roysh, and then Angel goes, "Oh my God, I don't have any money", and Oisínn tells her not to worry, that he'll get it, and Ana with one n asks him to get her a Whopper with cheese while he's up there.

When he's gone, Angel goes, "Oh MY God, I cannot BELIEVE you are getting a Whopper with cheese. Do you ACTUALLY know how many points that is?"

Ana with one n is there, "No", and Angel goes, "It's, like, thirteen-and-a-half. You've already had garlic bread today, which is, like, three-and-a-half, and a bag of popcorn, which is two, and chocolate mousse, which is also two. Oh, and a bowl of Special K. Honestly, you ACTUALLY have no willpower."

Ana with one n goes, "Look who's talking, you had garlic bread, a bag of tortilla chips, a creme caramel..." Angel goes, "Yeah, and now I'm having fries and a Diet Coke, which adds up to 15 points. Which means I've got nine saved up for tomorrow."

Ana with one n shrugs her shoulders and goes, "I'm thinking of doing that Russian Airforce Diet that Sophie was talking about", and Angel goes, "It doesn't matter what you do. You have ABSOLUTELY no willpower."

Oisínn comes back, roysh, and says the queue was, like, totally mental. Ana with on n says that they're going to have to stort letting all the refugees work in places like McDonalds and Burger King, because they just can't the staff anymore.

She's like, "It's the Celtic Tiger".

Angel goes, "Tell me about it. My mum CANNOT get a domestic. Can you believe that?"

Ana with one n asks how I've been and listens while her burger goes cold and untouched on the table.

* * * *

It's, like, half-ten in the morning, roysh, and the old man's cor is still in the driveway, and it's obvious there's something wrong. I go downstairs, roysh, wearing a black Russell Athletic t-shirt and Calvin Klein boxer shorts, and he's on the phone, presumably to *The Irish Times*, because he's got the sports page open, and he's totally freaking the head. We are talking totally here.

He's just there going, "I want to speak to Malachy Logan... NO, HE DOESN'T KNOW WHAT IT'S IN CONNECTION WITH, BUT HE BLOODY WELL WILL IN A MINUTE".

Malachy Logan mustn't be in, roysh, because the old man is like, "Well, when he comes in, would you please ask him how the HELL *The Irish Times* can justify giving 14 paragraphs to the St David's versus Blackstones College match yesterday when they only gave nine to Castlerock's victory over Queen's Hos last week." Then he, like, slams down the phone.

I go pour myself a cup of coffee, roysh, and he goes, "Good luck today, Ross. Or should I say, 'Go raibh an t-adh leat'".

I'm there, "Yeah, whatever", and I bring my coffee upstairs to my room.

I go to my drawer and take out my Creatine and pour about 30 grammes into my mug. I have a shower and get dressed in between sips. I put on a grey jumper with a black neckband by Tommy Hilfiger, grey trousers by Sonnetti, brown docksiders by Dubarry and a navy sailing jacket with red fleece lining by Henri Lloyd. I have two messages. Elinor phoned and said sorry she didn't wake up that morning, that she was SO out of it, that her hangover the next morning was, like, SO bad, and that she wanted to wish me luck in my oral Irish. The second message is from Ana with one n, who wanted to know whether I had, like, my oral Irish this morning and if I did she hoped I'd do well. She said it might sound corny, but she knew that I could do absolutely anything I wanted if I really put my mind to it. She also sent me a text message, which is like, "GOOD LUCK BABY. CALL ME LATER".

I wait until the old man leaves the house, take the Lexus and drive up to the school. I check my watch and I've got, like, 20 minutes before I'm due to go in. I am SO not ready for this. I go into the jacks, roysh, lock myself into one of the booths, take out my creatine and pour about 40 grammes out onto the top of the cistern.

I use my credit cord to break it up into lines, roysh, then realise that I've got nothing to snort it through, so I go back out into the corridor and there's, like, a flier on the noticeboard telling us that auditions for Oklahoma, the musical we're supposed to be doing with the Mounties this year, are on Thursday at four o'clock in the assembly hall. I pull it down, tear off a decent-sized corner, go back into the jacks, roll it up and snort four or five lines.

I head down to, like, B6, where the orals are going on, roysh, and I am totally buzzing. I'm, like, up in the clouds, and I stort getting this, like, fit of giggles, roysh, and I just can't stop. Anyway, roysh, this total focking granny opens the door, roysh, and says my name in Irish, and it takes me ages before I cop that she's calling me. I go in, roysh, and sit down and she's like, "So, conas atá tú?"

I'm, like, trying to hold in the laughter.

She goes, "Conas atá tú, an bhfuil tú go maith?"

And I go, "Voulez vous coucher avec moi, ce soir?" and stort breaking my hole laughing.

She is SO not amused, roysh, but the more I sit there, looking at her in her cardigan and tweed skirt, and a face like she's been sucking a lemon, the more I laugh and, like, I just can't stop, so after about five minutes I just get up and leave.

As I'm going out the door, I turn around and go, "May nim ees Ross O'Carroll-Kelly", and then burst my shite laughing again.

* * * *

Fionn sees the white powder on, like, my jumper and storts looking at me suspiciously. Last year, of course, he wouldn't have noticed it, because we had, like, a grey jumper, the same as the rest of the school. This year, all the goys on the S are wearing a black one. Fionn is, like, staring at me and I'm there, "Sorry, have you got a problem?"

Fionn goes, "No, but I think you have".

I'm like, "What are you, a focking doctor or something?"

He goes, "No, but I know enough not to touch that shit. They don't know what side effects it can have".

I grab him the scruff of the neck and pick up a bottle, roysh, and

I'm like, "I'LL SMASH THIS THING INTO YOUR FOCKING FACE".

Simon, Oisinn and Rory have to, like drag me off him, and then Simon tells me I am SO out of order and I should go for a walk and sort my head out. Everyone in the sixth year common room is just, like, staring at me, so I just, like, walk out.

I know I've got a major creatine problem but that's not ACTU-ALLY the reason why I'm dying to kill someone. The real reason is because I've got, like, piles, roysh, and they are SO sore it's unbeliev-able. I thought I was going to die yesterday. We beat Booterstown College 29-19, roysh, but I had a total mare of a game, and we are talking TOTAL here.

I shouldn't REALLY have played and I though about faking, like, a hamstring injury or something, but I ended up, like, snorting some Creatine before I went out, just to try to, like, kill the pain a bit. It didn't work, though. I should have scored a try after, like, ten min-utes, roysh. I was, like, practically clean through and only, like ten yords from the line when one of their goys grabbed my orse as he tried to tackle me and I'm was there, "AAARRRGGGHHH!!!"

It was, like, SO sore, I was in total ribbons for the rest of the game. My kicking was SO bad that Conor had to take over from me halfway through the second half. He converted JP's second try and kicked four penalties to put us into the semi-final. I was, like, limp-ing off the pitch at the end, roysh, and Hazel Cronin-Colleary, this total babe who's, like, deputy head girl in Whores on the Shore, she comes over and goes, "Oh my God, Ross, what happened to you?"

I'm just there, "I think I ruptured my pancreas going for that try".

Actually, it wasn't, like, too bad, because I ended getting LOADS of, like, sympathy shifts, as Christian calls them, later on. I was with Hazel, who is SO like Andrea Corr it's unbelievable. I was also with Emma Ryan, who's, like, sixth year On The Green, and Eri-ka, her best friend, who looks a little bit like Mariah Carey. I am SO gagging for it these days, I'm getting as bad as Christian, who the goys call The Libido King.

Anyway, roysh, I seriously have to sort this problem out, so I walk down as far as the Merrion Centre and, like, go into the chemist. There I am, roysh, looking through all the various creams and shit, and I'm about to pick up a tube of Preparation H, roysh, when I feel this tap on my shoulder.

I turn around, roysh, and I'm like, 'OH MY GOD, TOTAL SHAMER', because it's Sorcha, and she goes, "Hi".

I'm like, "What are you doing here?"

She goes, "I'm working in mum's shop".

I'm like, "But why aren't you in college?"

She goes, "HELLO? I'm doing Orts, Ross. I only have to go in on two afternoons a week and for an hour on Friday mornings".

She looks really well. She's wearing a white shirt by Scott Henshall, a black wool shrug by Morgan, a black pencil skirt by Karen Millen and black mules by Gucci. She's also wearing Contradiction by Calvin Klein, which is new and I wonder whether she's going out with someone or seeing someone, and whether it's over between her and this Brandon Oakes retard, and whether she told him about being with me. But I don't ask because I wouldn't give her, like, the satisfaction of letting her think I give a shit one way or the other.

We're, like, chatting away there, roysh, and she says she's, like, really sorry about that night, that she acted like SUCH a skanger, but she was SO locked because her Melanie had gone for a quiet drink after hockey and ended up going on the total rip all day. I tell her it's cool, and then she goes, "By the way, what are you doing here? You're not buying haemorrhoid cream, are you?"

I'm like, "No. Actually I'm buying condoms", and I pick up four packets, roysh. You should have seen her face, she was, like, SO jealous. She's there, "I heard you're going out with Ana with one n".

I'm like, "Yeah, sort of".

Then she goes, "It's good to see that you're taking precautions these days".

I just smile at her and tell her I'll give her a call and, as I go to the counter to pay for the condoms, she goes, "Make sure it's not Tuesday night. I've got cello practice".

* * * *

LOOK AT THEM, ROSS. SCUM-SUCKING WHORES AT THE CORPORATE GANGBANG. Christian is doing the modern socialist movement as his special topic, roysh, and he's reading FAR too many of those, like, propaganda sheets that they sell outside the GPO on a Saturday afternoon. Although he does have a point, though. This place is, like, full of complete tossers. The old man had to go to the Cayman Islands for a few days, to see his solicitor, roysh, so he gives me his tickets for the Ireland and France game at Lansdowne Road, and they're, like, corporate hospitality ones.

He goes, "Enjoy yourself, Ross, and don't do anything to disgrace the family name... And by the way, I've already told your mother this, if the Gardaí call tell them I'm in Tenerife playing golf".

I'm just there, "Fine", and then I phone up Christian, roysh, and I'm, like, "YEAH, FREE DRINK". We meet at Sandymount Dorsh station, roysh, and walk down. I can tell from the way he's walking that Christian's been snorting creatine this morning, but I don't care because I have as well.

Once we get inside the ground, we find our tent pretty easily, and we stort knocking back the drink, and after, like, about an hour we are totally hammered. We stort, like, singing, roysh. We're there, "BYE BYE MISS AMERICAN PIE" and all these spas in suits are staring at us. Christian goes, "WHAT THE FOCK ARE YOU LOOKING AT?"

Then all of a sudden, roysh, they wheel out some spa who used to play for Ireland in, like, the Fifties or Sixties or something, roysh, and it's, like, a questions and answers thing. Everyone's like, "How would the team you played in fare against the Irish team of today?" and "Do you think professionalism has changed the game for better or worse?", which is, like, BORING.

I'm like, totally skanky at this stage, roysh, and I put up my hand and go, "Will Carling captained England to numerous Five Nations Championships and the semi-final of the World Cup, while knobbing Julia Carling, who's, like, a total babe, and allegedly Princess Diana, who was the most beautiful woman in the world and the future queen of England. The height of the average Irish player's ambition is a quick knee-trembler in the carpark at the back of the Wicked Wolf in Blackrock. Is that why we're shit at rugby?"

He doesn't answer, roysh, and everyone's just, like, looking at me and shaking their heads, and Christian goes, "WELL, AREN'T YOU GOING TO ANSWER THE FOCKING QUESTION?", but there's no time, because the match is about to kick off and everyone storts shuffling towards the exit and they're given, like, a cushion and hip-flask full of whiskey on the way out. Me and Christian don't bother our orses with the match, we just stay inside the tent, knocking back the drink and, like, using our rolled-up match tickets to snort a few more lines of Creatine. Next thing we know, roysh, the tent is full again and the game is over and it's, like, hot port for everyone.

Christian asks this spa who looks a bit like my old man what the score was and he goes, "Ireland lost 10-9. Very unlucky", and Christian goes, "Ireland always focking lose".

Then they wheel in a couple of players off the Irish team to talk about the game, roysh, but me and Christian are in the corner playing, like Chariots of Fire at this stage, using the foam from our cushions instead of toilet paper. For a laugh, roysh, Christian gets a glass of Sambucca and throws it over me and my orse just goes, "WHOOSH", up in flames, and then the whole tent catches fire.

We all have to, like, evacuate, roysh, and I grab one of the Irish players on the way out, I can't even see who it is I'm so hammered, and I go, "I have a question for you. How many times did you do the Leaving?" He does NOT find it funny.

7

...

THE doorbell rings, roysh, and I shout downstairs to the old dear that I'm not in if it's Ana with one n, but it's not her, and it's not Sorcha or Alyson or Keeva or Jayne either.

The old dear is there, "Oh my God, it's Al and Kay Guy", and I can hear her telling them that I can't give a sample because I'm pregnant. Then old man arrives out into the hall and tells the old dear to leave the talking to him, and then he says to the Guys that I'm already the most tested schools rugby players in the world and you only have to look at me to know I'm not on drugs. Then I wake up. My white Russell Athletic t-shirt is, like, soaking, and we are talking totally here. I go into a bathroom and cut a few lines of creatine using a concession from a nightclub I may or may not have ended up in on Saturday night.

I have four messages. Elinor phoned to remind me that I haven't returned her last five calls and to tell me that I'm SUCH an asshole and a TOTAL dickhead and everything that everyone says about me is, like, SO true.

Hazel called and wanted to know whether I really meant what I said that night because she's been doing quite a bit of thinking and she thinks she feels the same way, and then she says good luck in the match today.

Angel phoned to say she has tickets for The Lighthouse Family if I'm interested and I should call her because we SO need to talk. Ana with one n phoned to say that Angel is SUCH a bitch, because she's making her feel guilty for having a packet of Hula Hoops, which is, like, three-and-a-half points, but she has a point, she supposes, because that was on top of a bap, which is, like, four-and-a-half points, with cheese and coleslaw, which is, like, God knows how many, a Heinz Weight Watchers vegetable and pasta medley, which is five-and-a-half, garlic bread, which is, like, three-and-a-half, two bottles of Lucozade, which are two-and-a-half points each and about ten or eleven or her old dear's After Eights, which are, like, half a point each.

She goes, "Can you BELIEVE that? One After Eight is half a point?" She says she has SUCH a pain in the orse with the whole thing that she might just end up doing the Montignac diet or maybe the Scarsdale one and she SO doesn't care what Angel thinks, the anorexic bitch. Then she says she'll see me at the match and wishes me luck.

I go downstairs and the old man is, like, sitting at the table in the kitchen, opening the post. He gets up when he sees me, roysh, and asks whether I want coffee.

I'm like, "Yeah".

He fills the kettle and then puts four scoops of Bewley's freshly ground medium roast into the plunger. I get up and put, like, 15 grammes of Creatine in on top of it, and the old man considers saying something but then thinks better of it.

He just goes, "I'm taking the whole day off work to go to the match, Ross. I'm even going to turn the mobile off."

I'm like, "YIPPEE", and he goes, "Please show me some respect, Ross".

Then he storts going on about how he's just been onto morkeshing department of *The Irish Times* and how he's going to be, like, sponsoring the schools rugby coverage in future and they're going to give it, like, two pages.

He's there, "It's going to be a bit like their 'Bulmers Total Golf' section, except it's going to be called 'Total Schools Rugby Totally', or something like that, we haven't worked out the finer points yet, but isn't it exciting? And part of the deal is that Gerry Thornley HAS to cover every Castlerock match."

I'm like, "WOW". He makes a couple more efforts to get all palsy-walsy, but I just, like, totally blank him and eventually he just gives up. As I'm going out the door, he goes, "One game away from the final, Ross. I will be so proud of you if you win today."

I'm like, "You are SUCH a spa".

I arrive at the school at, like, 11 o'clock and there's, like, major shit going down. We are talking MAJOR here. Sooty has been sacked as coach of the S for claiming, in an interview with the school magazine, that people who live in local authority houses are paying for the sins of a previous life.

Feely calls all the team together, roysh, and goes, "I know that a great many of you will sympathise with Mister Sutton's views. God knows, I do, but sadly in this age of political correctness gone mad it is not always prudent to articulate those views in public. Unfortunately, our sponsors took this view, worried as they are about their profile in poorer, working class areas, where apparently their sales are particularly high."

He tells us, roysh, that Sooty is staying at the school and will be taking over as, like, director of rugby, and our new coach is this New Zealand goy called Kenny East, who's supposed to have had trials with the All Blacks back in, like, the 'Sixties or something.

He gives us a bit of a speech in the dressing-room before the match, but it's, like, SO not the same, and when Simon stands up to make his speech, roysh, he just goes, "LET'S FOCKING WIN THIS THING FOR SOOTY", and we all go totally ballistic, roysh. We're all, like, stamping our studs off the ground, kicking the lockers, banging the walls, and Kenny East is there going, 'Oh MY God, what the fock have I got myself into here'.

Benedict's have a really good side this year, roysh, but we are SO up for this game they have, like, NO chance. Christian scores two tries right under the posts in the first, like, eight minutes, roysh, and I add the points, and we're, like, 23-12 up at half-time. We go in, roysh, and Kenny East's about to stort, like, telling us what to do in the second half, when all of a sudden, roysh, Simon get up and, like, pushes him out of the way, and goes, "Sorry, I'm taking over this team talk. Listen, goys, just go out there in the second half and think of Sooty. Remember him hammering on the floor and urging us to channel our nervous energy properly. Remember him leading us into yet another chorus of *Castlerock Above All Others*. Remember him bursting his orse helping to get us to the final last year and how we let him down by losing the final. Let's make sure we get back to Lansdowne Road so we can make amends. Let's do it for HIM."

We go back out, roysh, and totally ace the second half, and we are talking totally here. Simon and Fionn both get tries, which I convert. All the Benedict's supporters are there going, "ROSS IS A JUNKY, ROSS IS A JUNKY", but I have, like, the last laugh in injury time, roysh, when one of their backs, a total retard, drops the ball and I get over for a try. For my celebration, roysh, I get down on my hands and knees and stort snorting the try-line, and all their supporters are going, like, totally ballistic.

After the game, roysh, Ana with one n comes up to me, roysh, and storts, like, hugging me, and I am SO not in the mood for this shit. She looks quite well in a pink Ralph Lauren shirt with the collar up, black jeans by Hobo, black penny loafers by Next and a royal blue sleeveless bubble jacket with yellow fleece lining by Tommy Hilfiger, but all the goys on the team are, like, total babe magnets at the moment, and this is one night of the year that I want to be, like, young, free and single, and we are talking totally.

I just turn around to her, roysh, and I'm like, "I don't want to go out with you anymore."

She goes, "Sorry?"

I'm like, "I'm ending it."

She's goes, "Oh my God, you've done the dirt on me, haven't you?"

I'm like, "I ACTUALLY haven't stopped doing the dirt on you. I was even with, like, Angel, your so-called best friend".

I walk away then, roysh, and go back the dressing-room and even though I've got my back to her, I can tell she's, like, still standing there with her mouth open.

*   *   *   *

TALKING ABOUT ME AGAIN? The old dear totally kacks herself when she sees me, roysh, and she's ACTUALLY going to deny it, when the old man stands up and goes, "Your mother and I are worried about you, Ross?"

I'm there, "Really?"

He goes, "Yes. You're quiet, moody, irritable. You're showing all the classic signs of someone who's on.... I'm going to have to come out and say this... on drugs."

The old dear goes, "Things have been going missing from the house as well, Ross. The crystal carriage clock that your father and I got for our 25th wedding anniversary. The John Rocha napkin holders..."

The old man goes, "My golf trophy".

I'm there, "What golf trophy?"

He goes, "The one I won at the Pro-Am in Portmarnock, playing with Ronan Collins and Christy O'Connor junior. It's gone, Ross."

I'm just like, "And you think I stole all this stuff". The old man's like, "No, we just want to find out what's been troubling you lately".

I go totally ballistic then, roysh. I'm like, "Look, I'm not the criminal in this family. I'm not the one who keeps flying off to Jersey and the Cayman Islands to meet accountants and solicitors and shit", and then I turn to mum, roysh, and I go, "And YOU. I'm surprised you notice anything around here. I though you were too busy with your Ban Poor People From The National Gallery campaign".

She goes, "That is not what we're about, and well you know it. We simply feel that if they're going to allow school children in, they should be a bit better behaved and not let run amok. One morning a week, that's all me and the other girls want."

I look at her with, like, TOTAL contempt and go, "You and your focking coffee mornings".

She storts crying then, roysh, and she's there, "We could end getting head lice off these children, is that what you want?"

I just go, "When was the last time either of you knew what I wanted?", and even though I don't know what I meant by that, it sounded kind of good, and then I just, like, storm out the room.

I go upstairs, have a shower and put on a red and white striped rugby shirt by Ralph Lauren Polo Sport, navy chinos by Dockers and blue and red docksiders by Dubarry. I have four messages, but I don't bother my orse checking them. I just phone Angel and tell her we SO need to talk and we arrange to go for something to eat in, like, the Chicago Pizza Pie Factory.

I'm on the way out the front door, roysh, and the old pair are still, like, talking about me. The old man's going, "I think it's these blasted mobile phones. The atmosphere is so full of these, whatever they're called, electromagnetic waves. I was talking to Doctor

O'Kennedy at the regatta at the weekend and he was saying that getting on the 46A bus into town these days is the equivalent of putting your head in a microwave over for seven-and-a-half minutes..."

Angel says I am SUCH an asshole for telling Ana with one n about me and her being with each other and she says she just, like, denied everything. I tell her that I just couldn't take, like, the lies anymore, which is total bullshit, and Angel says she feels SO bad because Ana with one n is SUCH a good friend, which is also bullshit. I know this because I tell her that I want to be with her tonight and she says she SO wants to be with me as well. She looks totally amazing tonight. She's wearing a white halter-neck top by Elle, a fuchsia satin shirt by French Connection, which is unbuttoned, charcoal grey trousers by Amanda Wakeley and black boots by Gucci. She's also wearing fake tan, judging by her darker than normal colour and the amount of the stuff that's managed to make its way onto, like, her halter neck.

I order barbecued chicken wings, a Cincinnati chilli, a portion of fries and a Coke and Angel asks for a Greek salad with extra red onion and no feta. I ask Angel whether she's having a beer and she's like, "HELLO? Do you KNOW how many points that is? A pint is, like, three points", and she turns to the waitress and goes, "No, I'll just have some water please, non sparkling".

Then she goes, "Oh MY God, I was SO bold on Saturday night. I had four pints, roysh, which is, like, 12 points, and that was on top of a sweet and sour pork from the Chinese, which is, like, ten and OH MY GOD a tub of fromage frais, which is two, a packet of Tayto, which is, like, two-and-a-half, and a bowl of Special K, which doesn't really count because it's only, like, one-and-a-half".

My Choc Extravaganza arrives, roysh, and as I tuck into I'm like, "Where were you on Saturday night?"

She goes, "The rugby club. I know what you're going to say and you're right. It's, like, SO last year, isn't it? All the girls from Pill Hill were there on Saturday night. Oh my God, it was SO full of skangers."

I'm like, "Who were you there with?"

And she goes, "Ana", and she goes all quiet then, roysh, as though she's storted feeling guilty about something, but she gets over it pretty quickly, because she storts, like, feeling my leg under the table and she goes, "Do you think Courtney Cox's hair would suit me?"

* * * *

SHE COULD HAVE LOST HER EYE. Father Feely is going TOTALLY ballistic at us.

He's like, "IT'S DIFFICULT ENOUGH TO BELIEVE THAT CASTLEROCK STUDENTS IN THEIR FINAL YEAR WOULD BEHAVE IN THIS WAY, BUT MEMBERS OF THE SENIOR RUGBY TEAM".

Which is complete bullshit, roysh, because it happens every year and it's almost, like, a tradition at this stage. Me, Christian, JP and Oisinn bunked off double chemistry this morning, headed down to Pill Hill and ambushed these three total skangers with eggs and flour bombs. Apparently, one of them got hit in the eye and it's all, like, bloodshot, roysh, and the nuns went totally ballistic and phoned up the school.

Feely's there, "As you are all members of the Senior Cup team and the final is only three days away, we can put this little episode down to pre-match tension. You won't be punished this time and I'll send this girl's parents a solicitor's letter, just in case they go looking for damages. Fiends for compensation, their kind. But I have to warn you boys, that if you maliciously injure any other schoolgirls, you could face suspension, schools final or no schools final". Then he, like, smiles and gives us a little wink and tells us we can go.

We go outside, roysh, and I have high-five Fionn and Christian, and Oisínn high-five me and Fionn and, like, Christian high-fives us all. I go into the toilet, roysh, and using a cigarette lighter and a spoon, I cook up some creatine with some heroin and cocaine in a kind of speedball concoction. I suck it up into my works, roysh, then roll up my sleeve and, using my tie as a tourniquet, tap up a vein and put the stuff into me. I am, like, SO buzzing it's unbelievable.

I decide to bunk off for the rest of the day, roysh, and I go down for the Dorsh and head out to Sorcha's gaff in, like, Killiney. I am SO dying for my bit, roysh, and I'm going to give her the old 'I'm so nervous about this game, it's the biggest day of my life, you're the only one who understands' bullshit that they all love.

121

I arrive at the door, roysh, knock, and her, like, little sister answers it. I'm like, "Is Sorcha in?", and she goes, "No, she's at the orthodontist".

I'm like, "Will she be back soon?" and she goes, "About an hour".

I'm like, "Can I come in and wait", and she goes, "Sure".

We're in the hall, roysh, and she tells me Sorcha has her mobile with her and I can ring her from the kitchen if I want, but I'm like, "No, it's fine. I don't mind waiting."

We go into the sitting-room, roysh, and she's got, like, MTV on, and we just sit there watching it. A Robbie Williams song comes on, I think it's, like, *Strong*, and she says Robbie Williams is SO cool, and asks me did I see him interviewed on 2TV last weekend, and I say no, and she goes, "He's, like, SO mad".

I can't ACTUALLY remember her name, roysh, but it's, like, the first time I've ever looked at Sorcha's sister and realised how, like, good looking she is. She's, like, a Mountie, roysh, and I think she's in fifth year, but she has grown up SO much in the last year. She's wearing a black fur-collared cardigan by Morgan over a pink, a short-sleeved t-shirt by Kookai that I think I've seen Sorcha in before, beige combats by Hobo and blue and white chunky soled runners by Sketchers. She's also wearing Contradiction by Calvin Klein, which presumably she's also stolen from her sister's room. She's actually REALLY gorgeous, roysh, small, long blonde hair, pretty face, SO like Anna Kournikova it's unbelievable.

I'm like, "You used to play tennis out at Fitzwilliam, didn't you?" She goes, "Oh my God, how did you know that?"

I'm like, "I never forget a pretty face".

And she's, like, really embarrassed, roysh, but within five minutes I'm going, "All the time I was with Sorcha I was ACTUALLY thinking about you", and I end up being with her. She is SUCH an amazing kisser.

After about ten minutes of snogging, roysh, she all of a sudden jumps up and goes, "Roysh, I better get back to work".

I'm like, "Cool. Why aren't you at school this afternoon anyway?" and she goes, "I got the afternoon off to prepare my debate".

I don't even bother asking what the topic is. I just go out to the hall and I tell her that it's probably best if, like, Sorcha doesn't find out about this, and she goes, "Oh my God, totally. She would be SO pissed off".

I get the Dort as far as Dun Laoghaire, roysh, and the 46A home, and I'm in the door, like, five minutes when the mobile rings and it's, like, Sorcha.

She's going totally ballistic, going, "I KNEW YOU WERE A BASTARD, ROSS, BUT I CANNOT BELIEVE YOU WOULD DO SOMETHING LIKE THAT".

I'm like, "I don't know what you're talking about".

She goes, "She told me everything, Ross".

I'm there, "Who?"

She goes, "Afric".

I'm like, "Who the fock is Afric?"

She's there, "My sister. You were here this afternoon and you ended up being with her. She is SUCH a bitch, Ross. She only did it to get at me". She says I am SUCH a bastard and she should have listened to Melanie and then the line goes dead.

* * * *

St Aidan's are a bunch of total boggers who have no business being in the final of a competition like this. That's what Father Feely says.

He's like, "These people are muck savages. Not a lawyer's son between the lot of them. I don't think any right-minded person disagrees that their appearance in the final denigrates the entire competition. But they came through the various rounds to get there, and rules are rules, and until a better way is devised of stopping country schools from doing so well in the competition, we'll just have to put up with it. But you owe it, not only to your school, but to YOUR CLASS, YOUR PEOPLE, YOUR WAY OF LIFE, to ensure that EVERY SINGLE UPPER MIDDLE-CLASS one of you STANDS UP and makes himself counted this afternoon".

Then we all just, like, launch into a chorus of *Castlerock Above All Others*, roysh, and we just morch out of assembly in single file, with the cheers of our supporters ringing in our ears. They all stay on for, like, singing practice, roysh, because Kenny East said in an interview with Tony Ward that the famous Castlerock roar is like having a 16th man on the field, and Feely is holding up a copy of this morning's *Irish Independent* and he's going, "READ IT EVERYBODY. READ WHAT THE GREAT MAN HAS WRITTEN. READ IT AND WEEP ST AIDAN'S".

Kenny East, roysh, says he's watched video recordings of St Aidan's quarter-final and semi-final wins, roysh, and he tells us the various ways in which they're weak and then he, like, steps aside to let Simon make his motivational speech, which is, like, totally mind-blowing, better than any drug or controversial food supplement. He goes, "This is the biggest days of our lives, goys. We'll never be together like this again. When we leave Castlerock, most of us will go on to five-grand-a-term private colleges where we'll get qualifications without having to sit exams. We'll all get jobs through a goy we share a bar of soap with down at the rugby club and we'll shag all the little groupies who hang around the clubhouse until we reach our early thirties, when we'll marry the youngest, prettiest and thickest of these, and then continue to sleep with all of her friends. We all have bright futures ahead of us because we are the elite. But today is the last time we will eve have to work hord for anything in our lives. Let's make it count this year. Let's do it for Sooty. Let's do it for Castlerock. But most of all... let's do it for us."

When he finishes, roysh, I am, like, bawling my eyes out, and I look around the dressing-room and Christian, JP, Fionn, they're all crying. I am ready to walk through the focking wall for these goys, roysh, and we go out onto the pitch and, oh my God, I have never heard SUCH noise at Lansdowne Road, even for internationals.

The Aidan's goys are totally kacking it. You can see it in their eyes. I walk up to each one of them while they're, like, warming up, roysh, and go, "DEAD". They are SO bricking it. As a team, roysh, they're ACTUALLY worse than we thought. Fionn, Oisín and Christian all get tries in the opening 20 minutes, roysh, and we know than that we can, like, stort to relax and enjoy ourselves and we're, like, totall ripping the piss for the rest of the match. I kick two conversions and three penalties in the first half, and get both of our tries in the second, as well as two more penalties and one conversion, and we end up winning, like, 46-12. It is SO easy, roysh, and the Aidan's goys are SUCH bad losers. Their supporters are there, giving it the usual, "DADDY'S GOING TO BUY YOU A BRAND NEW MOTORCAR".

And our goys are like, "DADDY'S GOING TO BUY YOU A BRAND NEW COW". It's, like, SO funny. One of the boggers turns around to me, roysh, and goes, "Your captain shouldn't even be playing. He's 25 or 26".

I'm just like, "Mucker". The final whistle goes, roysh, and we're all like, "WE FOCKING DID IT". All the goys are, like, bawling their eyes out and hugging each other.

Aidans go up to get their losers' medals, roysh, and I stand at the bottom of the steps and, when each one of them come back down again, I go, "Fock off back to Bogland". Then we go up to get the Cup of Simon's old dear, roysh, and he collects it and just goes, "FOR MUM. FOR DAD. FOR SOOTY. FOR ROCK. FOR GOD", and he holds it up, roysh, and the whole place just goes totally ballistic.

We go back down onto the field and do a lap of honour and then, like, Tony Ward comes up to me and asks can he have an interview. I'm just there, "Shoot".

He's like, "Okay, first of all, how do you feel?"

I'm like, "I can't really put it into words. This has been my dream for years. And today that dream became a realisation."

He goes, "I noticed you had a word with each of the Aidan's players as they came down the steps with their medals. What did you say to them?"

I'm there, "I just told them they had done themselves and their school proud, that all the people who said they had no right to be here today had been proven wrong and that it was ACTUALLY our toughest match of the whole campaign".

He goes, "Just finally, I suppose you and the goys will have a quiet night in tonight".

And I'm like, "Yeah roysh. As if".

* * * *

IS this a bad trip or an epiphianic moment? Is it the effect of smoking creatine until the early hours of the morning to try to come down off the high of winning the cup or is it a profound moment of revelation set to change my life irrevocably. I never considered myself capable of using such word before, but not they slip out as spontaneously and as unselfconsciously as my dick used to after seven or eight pints in the rugby club on a Friday night.

I'm in Fionn's house in Bray. It's seven o'clock in the morning. All the goys are asleep on the floor of his old man's study, but I've been awake since four. My head was spinning, my bones felt like they were locked in a vice and the stomach cramps were almost too much to bear. For some inexplicable reason, I struggled to my feet and made my way towards Fionn's father's bookshelves, from where I plucked a copy of E M Forster's 1936 collection *Arbinger Harvest*. While suffering the horrors of withdrawal, I read the first essay in the collection, which was entitled Notes On The English Character. "The heart of the middle classes is the public school system," it said. "How perfectly it expresses their character.... With its boarding houses, its compulsory games, its system of prefects and fagging, its insistence on good form and *esprit de corps*, it produces a type whose weight is out of all proportions to its numbers. And they go forth into a world that is not entirely composed of public-school men... but of men who are as various as the sands of the sea; into a world of whose richness and subtlety they have no conception. They go forth into it with well developed bodies, fairly developed minds and undeveloped hearts."

This blew my mind. Even in my junk sick state, I could see what E M Forster was saying about the futility of my upper middle class, élitist existence. I read and read and read, absorbing his lesson greedily, but still I hungered for more. I returned to the shelf as the sun announced itself through a crack in the curtains, and I took Cyril Connolly's *Enemies of Promise*, and learnt its 'Theory of Permanent Adolescence' off by heart.

At about midday, Fionn wakes up and notices the book. "What the FOCK are you doing?" he says.

"I've been sucking on the teat of knowledge," I tell him.

"But you're reading, like, a book and shit. And what's happened to your voice. you've stopped saying roysh, like, and totally."

"I know," I say. "But what are those words other than crutches for lame minds."

Fionn gets angry then. He wakes all the other lads up and Simon decides there's enough evidence for me to face kangaroo court. I don't care. I'm still underlining interesting passages from EM Forster when Simon asks me to explain myself. "Have you ever heard of Cyril Connolly?" I ask him, wiping puke off the sleeve of my sailing jacket.

"Cyril Connolly?" he says, looking puzzled. "What school does he go to?"

I ignore this in the interests of educating the boy. "His Theory of Permanent Adolescence goes thus: 'It is the theory that the experiences undergone by boys at the great public schools, their glories and disappointments, are so intense as to dominate their lives and to arrest their development. From these, it results that the greater part of the ruling class remains adolescent, school-minded, self-conscious, cowardly, sentimental, and, in the last analysis, homosexual'."

Simon gets very angry. "Are you calling me a faggot?" he asks, animatedly.

"I'm saying that latently we're all homosexuals."

Simon just shakes his head and says, "Then you die".

"Everyone dies," I tell him. "But not everyone lives."

They all grab me then and, while singing the school song, they strip me, put a crown of shaving foam around my head, cast lots for my light blue Ralph Lauren shirt, tan coloured Armani cords, brown Dubarry docksiders and navy Henri Lloyd sailing jacket. Then they make me perform press-ups naked in a puddle in the garden and subject me an involuntary round of Chariots of Fire. I can feel my buttocks getting hotter as the length of toilet paper slowburns its way towards my sphincter, but I don't care. They can't break me and eventually I just conk out, tired, bruised and bloodied, but a new man.

* * * *

I wake up and my head is, like, SO wrecked, and I'm, like, totally naked, roysh, except for my Calvin Klein boxer shorts. I'm, like, covered in mud, roysh, and there's a piece of burnt toilet paper sticking out of my orse. I feel my face and there's, like, shaving foam all over it and my eyebrows have gone. I look up, roysh, and all the goys are standing over me, giving me daggers.

I'm like, "What's wrong, goys", and they just carry on staring at me, as though I've, like, done something wrong.

And I'm like, "Goys?"